The DataOps Revolution
Revolution
Delivering the Data-Driven Enterprise

The DataOps Revolution

Delivering the Data-Driven Enterprise

Simon Trewin

CRC Press
Taylor & Francis Group
Boca Raton London New York

CRC Press is an imprint of the
Taylor & Francis Group, an **informa** business

First Edition published 2022
by CRC Press
6000 Broken Sound Parkway NW, Suite 300, Boca Raton, FL 33487-2742

and by CRC Press
2 Park Square, Milton Park, Abingdon, Oxon, OX14 4RN

© 2022 Taylor & Francis Group, LLC

CRC Press is an imprint of Taylor & Francis Group, LLC

The right of Simon Trewin to be identified as author of this work has been asserted by him in accordance with sections 77 and 78 of the Copyright, Designs and Patents Act 1988.

ISBN: 978-1-032-10893-3 (hbk)
ISBN: 978-1-032-06296-9 (pbk)
ISBN: 978-1-003-21979-8 (ebk)

Trademarks Used in This Book

Contents

List of Figures

Acknowledgements

I would like to thank many people for the opportunity to write this book. First and foremost, my family, Sarah, Joshua, and Toby, who have supported me on the writer's journey.

I got into data systems early in my career, and I have never looked back. During that time, I have picked up tips, tools, knowledge, and experience from many people. This is divided into technical, architectural, personal, cultural, and organisational skills. Delivering data solutions requires skills in all these areas, and it would be hard to mention everyone on that journey. If you were part of that path, then thank you for working with me and providing the guidance and advice.

I would like to acknowledge the many influences I have been given over the years through reading numerous books. The DataOps Revolution contains many techniques that were first described by others. It has been my privilege to learn from these experts in their fields, applying them to my experiences and writing them into this story and the design of the Six IMPACT Pillars.

I started my journey in data at University, winning the Addison-Wesley Prize for computer science and receiving a copy of *The Relational Model for Database Management* by Edgar F. Codd.[1]

I progressed to building data systems for warehousing financial data in the big banks, and a big influence was *The Data Warehouse Toolkit* by Ralph Kimball and Margy Ross.[2]

I had huge success rolling out Kimball warehouses for years but needed a better way to store the data in the pipeline, leading up to the analytical schemas

---

[1] Codd, E. F. (1990). *The Relational Model for Database Management*. Version 2. Addison-Wesley Longman. ISBN: 0201141922.

[2] Kimball, R., Ross, M. (2013). *The Data Warehouse Toolkit: The Definitive Guide to Dimensional Modeling*, 3rd Edition. Wiley. ISBN: 9781118530801.

which brought me to *Building a Scalable Data Warehouse with Data Vault 2.0* by Daniel Linstedt and Michael Olschimke.[3]

Building automation into the pipeline required me to learn from the DataOps pipeline automation gurus in *The DataOps Cookbook* by Christopher Bergh, Gil Benghiat, and Eran Strod.[4]

The style of this book aligns to the story method of writing, and I first really enjoyed another Addison-Wesley Prize book, *The Mythical Man-Month* by Frederic P. Brooks, Jr.[5] This was followed by some suggestions from management gurus Ken Blanchard and Hal Burrows in *The One Minute Manager Meets the Monkey*[6]; *The Five Dysfunctions of a Team* by Patrick Lencioni[7]; and most recently *The Phoenix Project* by Gene Kim, Kevin Behr, and George Spafford[8] and *The Unicorn Project* by Gene Kim.[9]

I would like to acknowledge the many influences that I have had to help to describe what are some very complex ideas in everyday language and imagery. Simon Sinek's *Infinite Game*[10] is an excellent explanation of data processes that are infinite games played out by finite budget holders.

Finally, I would like to thank Andy Harrington for his excellent speaker's academy and his Tri-Summit Story Telling System and Coaching.

I hope that this style of book really gets you excited about implementing your data projects in a way that brings the joy back to the process of building data and analytics systems.

---

[3] Linstedt, D., Olschimke, M. (2015). *Building a Scaleable Data Warehouse with Data Vault 2.0.* Morgan Kaufmann. ISBN: 9780128026489.

[4] Bergh, C., Benghiat, G., Strod, E. (2020). *The Data Ops Cookbook: Methodologies and Tools That Reduce Analytics Cycle Time While Improving Quality.* Kindle.

[5] Brooks, F. P. (2013). *The Mythical Man-Month: Essays on Software Engineering.* Addison-Wesley.

[6] Blanchard, K., Oncken, W., Burrows, H. (1985). *The One Minute Manager Meets the Monkey.* HarperCollins. ISBN: 9780007116980.

[7] Lencioni, P. (2002). *The Five Dysfunctions of a Team: A Leadership Fable.* Jossey-Bass. ISBN 978-0-7879-6075-9

[8] Kim, G., Behr, K., Spafford, G. (2013). *The Phoenix Project: A Novel about IT, DevOps, and Helping Your Business Win.* IT Revolution Press. ISBN: 9781942788294.

[9] Kim, G. (2019). *The Unicorn Project: A Novel about Developers, Digital Disruption, and Thriving in the Age of Data.* Kindle. ISBN: 9781942788768.

[10] Sinek, S. (2019). *The Infinite Game.* Portfolio. ISBN: 9780241295595.

About the Author

 Simon Trewin is an IT professional and entrepreneur who has had the privilege of working with many leading organisations in delivering data solutions for over 25 years. He has a passion for data and analytics that has led him to structuring the Six IMPACT Pillars of DataOps, and he is the founder of the DataOps Thinktank on LinkedIn with 600+ members.

Simon is a regular speaker and presenter at data conferences and has published many articles on LinkedIn and social media. Key successes in his career have come from helping organisations to accelerate their data delivery using a combination of tried and trusted solutions and new thinking to enable them to meet challenging deadlines and overcome complex problems.

Simon has used DataOps techniques for the past 15 years. In that time, he has lead projects including:

- Successfully delivering data and analytics for a trading business through the financial crisis, enabling it to remain profitable throughout.
- Turning around a regulatory crisis at a large investment bank to deliver a solution in eight weeks that the bank in question had struggled with for six months.
- Building a team and delivering quality solutions to a large UK retail bank that satisfied a regulation within six months that was not being satisfied by a huge IT program.

The tools and techniques that he has learnt to achieve these outcomes are described in this book, and they are things that will improve how the reader implements successful projects with data and analytics. He has written this book to help people to make a step change in their capabilities.

Simon is co-founder and CEO of Kinaesis, which is the publisher of many articles in relation to DataOps. Kinaesis work with clients within financial services to leverage investment in data solutions and generate real value. Kinaesis have consistently achieved rapid success at a lower cost and risk for their clients in this complex and dynamic arena.

Introduction

In my experience working on, leading, and delivering many data and analytics solutions, it is building collaboration that has been the key to creating lasting, utilised, and innovative solutions.

The data world has evolved and is evolving at a huge pace, but the fundamentals of teamwork and shared responsibilities are the most important factors today, as they were in the past. It is the data sponsors who are as important as the technology experts and the chief data officers (CDOs). These visionaries are key to driving the solution and making sure that it gets implemented correctly. They take a share in the problem, and then they help to make sure that it delivers value.

The key to the success of IT professionals who work with data is to collaborate with your stakeholders. Work with them to create a shared vision, or help them see this vision to enable you to work towards a common goal. This is often the difference between success and failure. Without engagement there is no solution, without understanding there is no hope that you will build something that will be accepted by the people who are going to use it, and without empathy there is no mutual sharing of responsibilities and issue solving.

The best projects are those where the stakeholders work on solutions in tandem and deliver them together. In this scenario, small teams can achieve miracles that are deemed impossible by many looking on. In this flow state and shared vision, people put aside their egos and make the solution work. It has been my privilege to work on projects where we have been the small team defying the odds of delivery. Through this experience, I have learnt the art of building flow and collaboration where there has been none originally. My teams have been sought out for this ability over the years to take ownership of complex projects, and they have been able to deliver game-changing solutions where others have failed.

Over the years, and through working with our amazing clients, I have distilled what I know into a series of steps, best practices, and processes that will help you with your data projects.

My experience is that there is not a single size that meets all possible problems, and assuming there is is a mistake that many in the data world make. From experience, people know the tried and trusted, and then they look to apply it to all possible scenarios, getting frustrated when it does not work.

To read this book, you need to think of the information presented as a methodology to define the science behind building data solutions so that you can take it and apply it to the problem that you are trying to solve. If you are looking for a shape from this book that fits all problems, then you are not understanding the concepts presented, and you should take a step back and widen your gaze. By doing this, you will see that quite often the solution is much simpler than envisaged but may take you out of your comfort zone.

You may see some of the scenarios presented in this book as trivial and obvious; however, they are exaggerations of mistakes that we have witnessed and turned around in the real world. These mistakes could have cost organisations millions of investment dollars and caused projects to fail. They were saved through the application of these best practices, tools, and techniques.

The approach presented in the book lines up to the Six IMPACT Pillars of the DataOps model that Kinaesis has been using through its consultants to deliver successful projects and turn around failing deliveries. The pillars help to organise your thinking and structure your approach to delivery. The pillars are further broken down into substeps describing how this can be applied in the real world. If you want to know more about the Six IMPACT pillars, visit the Kinaesis website, where we store our news articles:

https://www.kinaesis.com

There is also a training site where you can learn the tools and techniques:

https://training.kinaesis.com

This book will be followed up with a more prescriptive technical book in 2021/2022. This will describe the six pillars in more detail and how Kinaesis uses accelerators and templates to structure their work.

To learn more about DataOps and join the revolution, there is the DataOps Thinktank. Many industry leaders write articles on DataOps, and we look to consolidate them in this group:

DataOps Thinktank | Groups | LinkedIn

I would like to thank you for purchasing this book and taking the time to read about DataOps and how it can help you to improve your data practices.

Why a Narrative Style of Writing?

Why did I choose a narrative style of writing for delivering what is largely a technical subject? The easy answer to this is that it is a style that I have enjoyed over the years, from reading *The Mythical Man Month*[1] at university to being advised to read *The One Minute Manager Meets the Monkey*[2] when I was learning my trade as a people manager. Each of these books and the lessons learnt from them still resonate in my head, and I still remember the key messages. They are also very easy to read.

Looking at this more deeply, storytelling has been a way to pass on knowledge and important information for thousands of years. Cave men drew paintings on the walls to pass on knowledge to future generations, and throughout human history, from the Greek myths to the Bible, humanity has continued to pass on knowledge using storytelling, fables, myths, and old wives' tales.

I wanted my story about data to reach as many people as possible and for people to understand the power of information and insight. I have experienced firsthand how access to the right data at the right time and the means to model it has enabled the businesses that I have served to reduce risk, make the right decisions, and take advantage of the opportunities in front of them. It has enabled teams to have more confidence in the work that they are doing and acted as a motivational tool.

The DataOps Revolution is a breakdown of these lessons and the knowledge that I have gained, presented in the form of a story. I hope that it acts as inspiration for many to move forwards in the right way and to get to productivity and value with their data more quickly and efficiently than they would do without it.

Background

The Saturn Banking Group has been navigating the financial markets since the 2007 crash. Like many organisations in its field, it was dealing with huge demands on producing report after report for the various regulations that the governing bodies required. At the same time, they needed to trim back on costs to fit the new world. They had already sold off a large chunk of their underperforming assets and were fitting the balance sheet up to be the right size for the more constrained operating environment.

---

[1] Brooks, F. (1975). *The Mythical Man-Month*. Addison-Wesley.
[2] Blanchard, K., Oncken, W., Burrows, H. (1985). *The One Minute Manager Meets the Monkey*. HarperCollins.

The executives of the firm were more nervous than ever about the real position of the organisation. They did not want to get caught out by any surprises. This put huge emphasis on the production of quality numbers and consistent key performance indicators (KPIs) that they could stand behind and support.

The group was formed over many years through acquisitions and mergers to be the size that it now is. Size in the financial markets is of huge benefit when you want to deal with large, complex transactions. This is not free of charge—the complexity of the underlying systems and data is huge. Large legacy processing systems still hold agreements dating back many years. They work perfectly well for processing transactions and collecting and making payments, but they are difficult to understand and complex to extract information from. Many of the original engineers have left the organisation, leaving few people who understand how these systems still work.

The complexity is not helped by the pressure in producing regulatory reports. There is neither appetite to build a large system nor the time to complete one, and previous attempts have not gone well. It is considered too risky and likely to cost many times the estimates that are conservatively passed around. The decision is that each regulatory delivery would have to be tackled in its own way, with a team in place to focus on it.

The technology landscape is not helping their cause. The bank had invested heavily in appliances to provide the storage and querying capacity to consolidate its data, only to find that huge amounts of technical effort and resources were being spent on data modelling and optimisation. It is harder to get engineers, as the world had moved on to bigger and better things like Big Data solutions and cloud technology. Technology innovation was moving fast, and as soon as the data lakes contained a copy of the legacy data, the world had moved on to cloud adoption. Mark Denby, CIO, is tasked with moving forwards confidently, with technology that continues to change under his feet.

The threat from disruptive technology is always on the horizon, and the need for digitisation has never been higher. Consumers are demanding information at their fingertips in real time to tell them exactly where they are and how much they can spend, save, or invest. To compete in this modern digital world, the bank would need to get more efficient at bringing data together and organising how it is stored and presented to be able to bring products and solutions to market to meet their customers' needs. The job is huge, and there needs to be a way to break it down and tackle it methodically.

The bank has gone through several reorganisations to try to get on top of the challenges that they are experiencing. The latest is the introduction of a lead of regulatory IT delivery. The role is born from the need to consolidate information consistently across many departments for supporting finance, risk, capital, and liquidity reporting. The regulator is asking for reports from all these areas and testing for consistency across calculations; therefore, it makes sense to consolidate this role.

The choice for filling the role will be complicated—the person will need many skills to manage the complexities and be able to deliver within a tough, complex, timebound environment. Mark Denby has been with the organisation for 15 years and knows the complexity involved. He is also aware that the current approach that they have been following is not getting results. He spends a lot of time with angry, frustrated business executives who constantly complain about the speed of delivery and the ability of the teams to understand what is needed.

Previous projects have failed to gain the support and the buy-in from the users, and they are considering the option of outsourcing the work to ease the pain. He is conscious that this is going to be a key position to stabilise the department and quieten the noise within the organisation. Within his ranks there are several key lieutenants who have worked hard for their place within his management team. Many have been loyal throughout the difficult period, and they have shared the trenches during the tough times, working many hours and through the night to make impossible deadlines.

The dilemma is that although this is great, he is not likely to change the dial in terms of ability to win back the business and regain the trust that they need to move forwards. He needs to make a bold move and embrace a new approach. He needs to take a different perspective on the problem that the department is facing.

He decides to look at the layer immediately below his lieutenants and find some new blood—someone who is achieving results and has a happy set of users and successful projects.

Jennifer Watson joined Saturn Banking Group four years previously; she has a quality CV and has worked in many business-facing IT roles at previous employers. She has quickly established her credibility within the bank with her business users. They seem to be happy and create little or no noise. For this reason, she is off the radar of the management team, who have been focusing on dowsing fires by working through the night. The heroes of the "firewatch" are some of the most respected managers.

Jennifer quietly goes about her business, delivering value and meeting the deadlines that are set. In the senior management circles, they put her success down to the ease of her position within the firm.

"The business is not particularly demanding," they say, and then get back to comparing the scars of their latest battles.

"She does not share our vision for the future; she only delivers unimportant increments to the users."

"She is not going to make the difference that digital transformation of the banking industry requires."

Jennifer has heard a lot of this before and is happy to be delivering value to her end users and maintaining her relationships. She realises that at the end of the day the bank is a bank, the users within the organisation are the only people who are in a position to know and manage the business landscape. She is therefore there to support them with expertise and skills to enable them to move forwards effectively.

It comes as a complete surprise when Jennifer is asked to attend a meeting with Mark Denby. She has attended his town hall meetings and met him at team-building meetings, but most of her engagement has been with her line manager. She entered the meeting nervously, not knowing what to expect. Has she done something wrong and is about to be told about it? That is not possible, as her department is running very smoothly, and her direct reports, in most cases, seemed very happy and productive. The business like her and are always backing her up with her managers, supporting her and singing her praises. She concludes that it must be something else.

Mark's office is in the corner of the IT floor. Sitting outside is his personal assistant. The office is glass, so you can see right in. The desk sits in the back right of the office, and there is a meeting desk in the office by the door. Mark has organised the office with a bookshelf full of technical, management, and business books. At the head of the desk is a large teleconferencing screen.

Jennifer entered the office after getting permission from Mark's PA and introduces herself.

"Hi, Mark, I am here for our 1 PM meeting."

"Hi, Jennifer, please take a seat. Can I get you something to drink?"

"No, I am OK, thank you."

"Jennifer, I would like to get to the point," Mark starts bluntly. "You joined the firm four years ago in risk IT, taking responsibility for aggregation and reporting. It is a tricky area that used to cause us huge difficulties; since you came aboard it has been turned around and is now an area that I need to spend very little of my time on. The users are happy, the team are productive and delivering results. The deadlines for projects are being met, and there are fewer outages and issues than there used to be."

Jennifer was still unsure where this was going, but the language seemed positive. "Thank you, a lot of that is down to my team and their efforts."

"Well, yes, that is true, but the team is the same team that you inherited when you joined. Some of it is down to the team, but I think a lot has got to be down to you," Mark said.

"Thank you, I do work hard, and I have been applying what I know from my years of working with some of the real data gurus," Jennifer said.

"I have a new challenge for you that I hope you will accept," Mark said, not beating around the bush. "As you know, we have been struggling with some of our complex regulatory deliveries across the organisation. We have had to request extensions, and the regulator is starting to lose patience with us.

"As you know, this has historically been split among the different business functions of the organisation, and therefore the delivery of reports has required huge amounts of coordination and duplication. On top of this, there is not a unified approach to producing data. The silly thing about this is that large quantities of the source data is the same across business areas, yet we have little standardisation, and we seem to continuously be reinventing the wheel. Our efforts over the past few years to create a single source of the truth seem to have tied us in knots, and it makes releasing anything difficult. I am concerned that we are losing credibility with the users, and I would like to turn the ship around."

Mark continued, "I have decided that to do this I need to think differently about the challenges. I need to put them under one person, and I need to pick that person based on a new set of skills and approach—someone who already seems to be making this happen. I think as a department we need to learn to approach things differently.

"I therefore would like to place that responsibility in your hands. I would like you to take your existing team and extend it to include members of the finance and treasury functions and to start to shape it to gain the results that you have been getting from the risk department. There are a number of crucial projects in this area that are required to hit regulatory deadlines, and missing them will cause great embarrassment to the firm."

Mark took a sip of his water. "I realise that this is a big step for you, so I fully expect that you will need to take some time with this. What are your thoughts?"

Jennifer obviously was taken aback. Although things were going well, she was not aware that her profile was high enough to be offered a role of this size. There were others who seemed to have a lot more presence in the department that she thought would be favored. She took a moment to gather her thoughts.

"Firstly, I would like to thank you for the offer. I very much appreciate your candor and the opportunity. Thinking on the spot, to do what I believe I must do, then I am going to need support from yourself to make the changes that I think are necessary. The work that we have been doing on a smaller scale in risk IT has been possible due to the support I have had from management and the business stakeholders. They have assisted me in driving the changes and the approach through and buying into it.

"There are many people in the finance, capital, and treasury functions who are happy doing what they are currently doing, and we will need to change the approach. I will need support to make sure that people are not given alternatives to the new approach. If we dilute what we are doing, then it will not happen," she continued.

"The second request would be to be provided with the time to assess the current setup and the project status and to be able to write up a plan of action before starting to make changes. I know this moves us closer to the deadline and does not move the team forwards, but I think I need to do justice to the people on the ground by understanding their unique challenges before we start to change things and move forwards again."

Mark thought this over. They were in a tight spot, and the deadline was looming, but he also needed to give Jennifer room to make a difference. "OK, I am happy with this, and you can rely on my full support for implementing what you need to do. The time for the assessment will take us closer to the deadline, which makes me nervous, but I appreciate that this is a big ask, and therefore you need to be confident in your actions."

"OK, I need a couple of days to think about the offer and the implications. Can I give you my answer after the weekend?" Jennifer asked.

"Of course, please make an appointment with Tina for Monday first thing," Mark said.

"I will," Jennifer replied.

With this, Jennifer left the office and set up an appointment with Tina for Monday morning.

• • •

Jennifer spent the weekend thinking through the positives and challenges of the offer. Despite the honor of being offered the role, she knew that it would be a lot of work and energy to be able to deliver on the program of work. She had seen the efforts of the team and knew that quite a lot would need to change for her to be able to build the level of productivity required to hit challenging deadlines. She thought back to what she had achieved throughout her career and drew strength from her previous successes. The answer was going to be yes; now she needed to get on top of her emotions to think it through carefully.

• • •

Monday morning came around quickly, and Jennifer was waiting promptly outside Mark's office. At 9:55, she entered the office. Mark had just completed his call with the IT leadership team in Asia.

"Good morning, Jennifer, I hope you had a good weekend," Mark greeted her warmly.

"Yes, thank you," Jennifer replied.

"Have you managed to think through the opportunity that I presented on Thursday and come to a conclusion?" Mark asked.

Jennifer got the impression that Mark knew the answer but needed to ask the question. "Yes, I would very much like to take this opportunity. I have thought long and hard over the weekend, and I think I am ready to take the next step. I believe that everything I have learnt in the past puts me in a good position to add value to the role, and I am ready for the next challenge."

"That is great news! I am really looking forward to working with you and having you part of the management team," Mark said.

He promptly got up and shook Jennifer's hand. She felt a little awkward, as things were moving fast. She thought to herself that he must be under a lot of pressure, as these things normally took a bit more time and preparation.

"How is this going to unfold?" Jennifer asked.

"Firstly, I would like to go through the team that will be reporting to you and the stakeholders. I can give you my insight and the backgrounds of the individuals," Mark said.

"Thank you, it would be good to set up sessions with them as soon as possible to understand where they are and to assess next steps," Jennifer responded.

"Let me start with the business. You know Brian Catts from your work in risk. He has been given responsibility for regulatory reporting across business functions. He is pulling together the verticals and trying to drive better business outcomes. He is a good sponsor of ours, although due to poor delivery he is under pressure from others within the business to find a better solution. He is willing to work with us to help turn things around, but he needs to show results as much as we do," Mark said.

"That sounds good; it makes all the difference with a strong business sponsor. I worked with Brian on a previous project, and he is willing to back you, but he expects delivery and is not the sort of person you want to let down. What are his major issues with IT?" Jennifer asked.

"The key issues are the speed of change and delivery. He is under huge pressure to produce reports and information for his management and the regulatory bodies. They each want their own format and structure, and none of it lines up to the way the business works. Each nuance of the reporting system is taking too long to build, so he has been forced to implement many end-user computing (EUC) systems. Each of these is implemented by separate teams, and they are producing results that are inconsistent. Secondly, his whole department has grown considerably since the crash, to the stage that people are starting to ask questions about its size. I have spoken to Brian about your appointment into the role, and he was fully supportive. To get a complete picture of the requirements, it would make sense to set up a meeting with him to discuss," Mark said.

"Yes, I agree. The first place to start must be the business team that we support. Without clear sponsorship and direction, projects will never get adopted, implemented, or declared successful. Who is responsible for the collection of user requirements and managing the change process with the business users?" Jennifer asked.

"That is Ian Cole, the change business analyst," Mark said.

"I know a little about Ian and his team; how is that going?" Jennifer asked.

"It is a difficult relationship that could work better. I think the challenge is that the team are analysts who understand the business and can articulate requirements, but they do not necessarily understand the IT. They therefore write down specified features and requirements that we have not got any hope of delivering. This just leaves the IT team always having to be the bad guys and saying it cannot be done.

"A lot of the IT team understand the business very well, so when they receive the specifications, they feel like they must rewrite them. The business analysts are useful in minimising the time that the business must spend with the team, but I do not think that it is the most productive process. The systems that we are building for the users contain very specific requirements that need to work a certain way and require open communication to be able to define the appropriate solution. The business requirements document (BRD) is not really working to anyone's advantage," Mark said candidly.

"I faced a similar problem when I first joined. The BRD process is really designed for teams that build applications. When it comes to data systems, the process is different. Over time, I changed the process around to be better suited to an analytics lifecycle. The act of producing analytics reports is very similar to producing regulatory submissions. I can use these same patterns working with Brian and Ian. If the team are producing BRDs, it sounds like we are very much working in a waterfall development process," Jennifer commented.

"They are supposed to be working to an agile process," Mark said skeptically. "They hold regular scrum meetings, with Sandra Cook coaching them through this. We break the BRD into user stories and epics, but due to the nature of the work, it seems like the team are going through the motions rather than implementing an agile project," Mark said.

"That would make sense—that is how data projects are!" said Jennifer.

"Do you mean that we cannot make them agile?" Mark asked.

"No, that is not what I am saying. The standard rules for agile projects do not apply to data projects as they do for building out web applications. Data is holistic; therefore, it is unlikely that you can produce the answers with only some of the data. This creates a challenge, which means that you need to understand how to iterate a data project effectively. A good relationship with the business is essential, as they need to buy into working in an agile approach, otherwise it is not possible to make progress. Who is responsible for the overall technical side of the project?" Jennifer asked.

"Justin Parkins is the technical lead and architect on the solution. He has got many years of experience at Saturn working on the financial ledger. He took up the role of technical lead and architect for the data and reporting platform two years ago and has been key to implementing the data lake. Since starting this project, we have been able to ingest lots of the data from the finance and ledger systems into the lake. He has delivered a couple of key business outcomes relating to the financial results.

"In the past few months, however, progress has become extremely bogged down, and each new request seems to be taking as long as the first requirement. We seem to have a large farm of data nodes, and it is tricky getting it to flex to the requirements we have. In addition to this, when we put together results from the lake, the users tell us the data is not reliable. I think he needs some help to be able to get back to efficient and effective delivery," Mark said.

"Is there a good understanding across technology and the business regarding the data in the lake?" Jennifer asked.

"The project and the CDO, Karen Lester, have led this and extensively documented the lake with dictionaries, models, and many sets of lineage documentation. We have thrown lots of money at this to meet the BCBS 239 regulation. We have more documentation than we know what to do with. The issue is not documentation but the speed that it goes out of date. On top of this, there seems to be a lack of adoption of the resources. People are still reinventing the wheel every time a project runs. The documentation, if anything, has created a bit of a chain around our neck and is reducing productivity," Mark said.

"This is the thing that does catch people out—how to leverage these resources effectively. They should be assets to the teams involved with data and enablers. On previous projects our data analyst teams have found the documentation and metadata invaluable to their progress. Who is leading the data analyst function?" Jennifer asked.

"Carl Hinkley has been leading this effort for us. Carl was a business analyst with a keen eye for data, so he was an obvious choice for leading the data analyst team. They spend a lot of time understanding the requirements and then turning them into data transformations. The challenge that we have is that a lot of what he produces does not seem to meet the requirements of the IT team or, when the solution is delivered, the business. The analysis is accurate, but often the requirement changes or gets clarified, invalidating the assumptions.

"The other issue is that the technology team take the information in the data specification too literally, and we end up with complications in the implementation and then a lot of debugging in the end solution. I think if this link in the chain can be made to work effectively, then we will be in a much better place," Mark said.

"OK, it sounds like there are quite a number of issues to address within the process and the project artefacts. I will probably have to work through this methodically by assessing the root cause of the problems, tackling the low-hanging fruit first, and then starting to build some momentum before I start to tackle the more complex challenges," Jennifer concluded.

Jennifer realised it was time to sum up. "It would make sense for me to meet with Brian Catts to understand his expectations and needs and see if we can do a level set with him to be able to target the biggest business wins to start with. Once they are feeling more comfortable, it should be a lot easier for us to build a more productive working relationship. I should then spend some time understanding what people are currently doing and then establish a plan of attack for tackling each area within the teams. Is Brian aware that I am his new person in IT for regulatory reporting requirements?" Jennifer asked.

"Yes, as mentioned, I have discussed your appointment with him, and he is very supportive. I will send him an email after this meeting and copy you in to say that you have accepted the role and that he should expect to meet with you soon. I will also send an email to the team and set up a meeting with them to announce your appointment and provide you with my support over the coming months. We should set up a one-to-one meeting on a weekly basis. Can you coordinate diaries with Tina to set this up and ask her to forward you an invite to the managers' meeting that happens every Friday morning? In the next session, I will introduce you to the rest of the management team," Mark concluded.

"OK, will do," Jennifer said as she got up to leave.

Tina was sitting outside Mark's office, and they coordinated diaries to put the one to one in on Tuesday mornings going forwards.

Jennifer took a few moments after the meeting to gather her thoughts and then put together a list of immediate actions. She checked her email; the messages from Mark sat at the top, and she would be meeting with her team tomorrow afternoon. She responded to Brian Catts off the back of Mark's email and set up a meeting for the morning. This would be a key meeting for her to build rapport and to start to understand the business drivers in more detail.

Part I

Scoping and Defining

Chapter 1

Setting the Vision

Key Concepts

When building data and analytics solutions, a large factor determining your success is the business sponsor and the work that you are carrying out meeting their needs. It is also likely that in low-trust environments prior to implementing DataOps, a shared vision of the direction of travel does not exist or is not accurate. Without understanding the true destination, you cannot be sure that the increment you are working on is taking you in the right direction. Successful projects are due to having a clear understanding of that destination or fighting to gain sight of it where it is not clear. Many people mistake agile for a free for all, where the destination of travel is determined every two weeks. In part this is true with regards to how you get there, but there needs to be a clear statement of the business goal to provide purpose. Many parts of the framework for a data project must be established over the longer term, and the shape of the framework is determined by the ambition of the vision.

J ENNIFER WAS targeting the key meeting with Brian Catts to build rapport and start setting up the foundations for creating collaboration between business sponsor, the users, and IT. A key building block of this was for them to have a clear sense of a defined, realistic, and achievable scope. Jennifer would need to use all her skill to be able to define this over the coming weeks with the business users, business analysts, and her team. Tomorrow was less about this and more about really understanding Brian's underlying target vision and to start to share the challenges that they would need to overcome in getting there. In Jennifer's experience, it was sometimes hard to get to this point in one meeting, given the amount of noise around the day-to-day activities. Understanding the noise would help her to get a picture of the issues and the challenges in the relationship, but the priority for the meeting with Brian was to talk about the big picture. To shape the meeting, she put together her agenda to send to Brian to contribute to.

- Introductions
- Background—Brian
- Immediate needs
- Scope for department / business
- Housekeeping—regular meetings, communication plans, etc.

She sent the agenda through to Brian and quickly turned her attention to reading the existing documentation for the project. This would take the rest of the day and some of her evening to read through. She needed to understand the status so she could prevent the meeting with Brian getting sidetracked and to instill confidence that she was coming up to speed quickly.

She downloaded the documentation onto her laptop locally to prevent her having to do this remotely, and she printed out some A3 sheets containing the project plans. She would head home early and then set up residence in her office and work through the information.

• • •

The morning came around quickly, and Jennifer arrived bright and early. The business floor was situated in a large, open-plan office on the second floor. The floor was laid out in a series of desks in groups forming logical team working spaces. Brian's desk was over on the south side with views out the window into the London skyline. Next to his desk was a glass office set out for team meetings and conference calls. The bank had global operations, and there was a need to regularly coordinate with colleagues in Asia and the Americas. The conference call with Asia was just ending, and the London attendees were filing out of the room to get on with their day's work.

Several faces were familiar to Jennifer as they filed past. Brian came out at the end and greeted Jennifer warmly. "Hi, Jennifer, great to have you onboard. I hope you have settled in OK. Could I get you a coffee or some water?"

Jennifer had had several coffees in the morning, so she thought a glass of water would be required over the course of the next hour. They quickly collected the drinks and made themselves comfortable in the office.

"Hi, Brian, thank you for taking the time with me this morning. I started in the role as IT manager for regulatory delivery yesterday, and I am greatly honored to be able to lead this programme. I look forward to working with you and the team over the coming weeks, months, and years. I believe that we can really move the business forward and help to integrate modern practices into the work that you do.

I sat down with Mark Denby yesterday, and he made me aware of some of the challenges that you have had over a period. I always like to meet with the business sponsor first, before anything else, to get a clear idea of the vision and scope of what we are looking to achieve. I will then join that up with the work on the ground. I find this allows me to understand the issues and to put them into context with the high-level vision. This is of real assistance and will help me to determine the best path forwards. Does that fit with your expectations?" Jennifer asked.

"That makes sense, although I have had this conversation with your predecessors lots of times in the past and we do not seem to make much progress. The team here are really losing patience with this process—they seem to talk to IT, then some grand plan gets launched, and then when it comes to deliveries nothing of substance comes," Brian said, struggling to contain his frustration.

Jennifer considered this for a couple of seconds and then responded. "The way that we need to set this up is to create a process of delivery that demonstrates value at intervals through the project lifecycle. We can then build back up the belief, trust, and momentum in the project," Jennifer replied.

"Ah, that would be agile. One of the project leads brought in that a few years ago, and little seemed to change," Brian said.

Jennifer realised there was going to be some work to do to build back the trust with the business. "I find that quite a lot with data projects. A standard agile approach does not work. What I suspect has happened is that the project team have not realised that there are only certain aspects of the project that can run agile. If you do not organise things correctly, then the agile process very quickly resorts back to a waterfall project. Part of the work that I will be doing initially is to identify this within the project plan then organise it to reintroduce agile. For this I will need to present to you and the team how this can work so that you understand our constraints and you can therefore help us to work with them. With agile there is a requirement for disciplined engagement and decision making and for us to be transparent with the blockers and the issues. Are you OK to work with me and the team in this spirit?" Jennifer asked.

Brian knew he needed results to be able to lift the morale of his team again. What had gone before had not worked. "Jennifer, of course I will work with you on this. We need to change approach, because what we are doing is not working!" he said bluntly.

"I will need a couple of weeks working with the team to understand where we are. In the meantime, they will be making progress on the immediate milestones, as this is key to make sure that we do not lose time against plan. Once I have had time to assess the current state, I will be in position to present back a set of recommendations and work through these with yourself and the other senior managers to prioritise them," Jennifer explained.

"I understand," Brian responded.

Jennifer sensed that Brian had calmed down from his initial position and was willing to move forwards, so she decided to move the conversation on. "Reading through the documentation there is a business case that states that the goal of the project is to build up a reliable source of data to be able to meet future demands and to improve the reporting process. Would it be possible to elaborate on this more so I can understand this from your perspective?" Jennifer asked.

"One of the big challenges that we have on my team's side is that there is a huge demand for information about the state of the business. This is coming from the regulators and senior management who are on the line for making sure there are no surprises. Passing each of these to IT is not feasible to meet the demands, even for new reports from existing data. We have employed many additional staff over the past few years to be able to meet the new demand, but the increase in costs is noticeable. I am having to reduce headcount whilst needing to produce more! Our attempts to build a central store and reporting engine has absorbed more resources than created efficiencies. I have resource dedicated to defining dictionaries, semantics, and business rules, but none of it seems to be making a difference.

"The IT team have produced a system, and it meets the requirements of one regulation, but when asked to add another, they seem to need to start again. On top of that, the data quality of what is produced is poor—meaning that my team must extract the data from the system and then massage it to be able to produce the reports that they need.

"These are the issues that are causing us the most problems, so my vision is to have a system that my team can use and work with that has source data and the means to cleanse it that is understood and easy to extend for additional requirements. The system should enable them to author reports and analyse data in a reliable and fast way. It needs to support full transparency and lineage to provide the management team with confidence to sign off on the results. This seems too big a step from where we are today, so we tend to go from requirement to requirement. If I gave this big mandate to IT, they would no doubt disappear for three years, and I would be left on my own to meet the immediate requirements," Brian said.

"I understand your perspective. I have found that if IT do not understand the target vision, they will build a system based on half the information available. When they do this, the first iteration of the system is not able to cope with the second requirement, because the architecture of the system has not considered where the requirements are going. This means they have to do lots of work to be able to turn the implementation around," Jennifer explained.

"So, you're saying that the delays in the IT system are my fault then?" Brian asked a little indignantly.

"No, that is not what I am saying! I believe that there needs to be a target that is out in the distance that provides a compass to the actions and iterations of the here and now. This is not aiming fault; it is just being able to set a course and then to define waypoints on the journey to that destination to measure if you are on track. As an analogy, think of a journey that you have taken in the past. If the destination were local shops, you would set up for this in a totally different way to if you are heading to the Arctic Circle on an adventure. The number of supplies and the choice of vehicle, clothing, and sleeping arrangements are totally different.

"If you tell someone that they are going to the local shops, and when they get there, you tell them that they are heading to the edge of town, and then when they get to the edge of town, you say they are heading to the next town, and so on, eventually you will run out of ability to go any further. This is where a lot of agile projects fail. They start with a list of current needs with no end in mind, and then the iterations that they take are not heading in a consistent direction, which means that they look like a random walk. This is OK if you have infinite resources and infinite time, but that is not the case. Each iteration must move you forwards towards your goal.

"We therefore need a business vision and the IT vision to line up with each other, and then we need to establish the route to the target, meeting the goals of the business and IT on the journey. At each step to achieve a goal, we may want to make a conscious choice to build something tactically, but there should be as much reusable collateral to move us forward at each step to enable the next phase to be easier," Jennifer said.

"I understand what you are saying, but how do we do this? Everything we do seems to get too big really quickly," Brian said.

"Firstly, we need to identify what can iterate quickly and what takes longer. Each part of a system will have different cadence or volatility, and you need to respect that cadence and work with it to be able to operate effectively. If you put a high volatility part of the system in the core of the framework that is supposed to be stable, then you end up with a lock, which means the system appears to grind to a halt," Jennifer explained.

"I am not sure I understand," replied Brian.

"OK, by way of example, in the reporting system the report formats change quite frequently—for example, the layout or the groupings in the report. If you put the definition of these format at the core of the system that other parts of the system rely on, then you cannot change them without all parts of the system downstream of these being tested. This takes considerable time and effort, so therefore only happens once every three months.

"If you put the definition of these as close to the end of the pipeline and near to the reports, you can change these frequently without needing to test anything other than the report itself. The secret of data systems is understanding the scope of data and then put it in the right place. Going back to the vision, to be able to make meaningful iterations, then we need to understand these things, organise them correctly, and then make sure all the placeholders are in position. This way we can give you what you need today and build up the picture towards the vision over time," Jennifer said.

"OK, so what you are saying is, we need to lay out the full vision for what we are going to need as a business and the roadmap of defined deliverables. You and your team will break that down into logical deliveries that satisfy the immediate deadlines, and then this builds to meet the target solution," Brian echoed back to confirm his understanding.

"Yes, and the breakdown of the system will be what we present back to you. There is a discipline that is required that recognises that if we need to take a shortcut for a deadline, then we are granted the time to reengineer the shortcut into a more robust solution. Typically, this is where it gets hard—if we are not allowed to do this, over time, we will slow down our deliveries, and the costs will go up," Jennifer explained.

Jennifer paused for a few moments to check if Brian had further questions before moving back onto topic. "To clarify the vision for the future, there is a number of questions that I need to ask you. Are you OK if I work through these?" Jennifer asked.

"Yes of course," Brian responded.

"How do you see the business working with the new system?" Jennifer asked.

"As you know, our primary focus is the delivery of information to support the control teams to oversee and help to facilitate the business. The emphasis in recent years, for obvious reasons, has been more on the control of the business—providing information to management and regulatory bodies to demonstrate that things are under control. The challenges that we are facing is the number of questions we are being asked at short notice go beyond our ability to respond. The market has been moving around a lot, and therefore people have been asking for different perspectives on the business.

"The second challenge that we are experiencing is that the regulators and management are wanting greater consistency between outputs. This creates pressure on us to make sure that the data is consistent, or if it is not for legitimate reasons, the inconsistency can be explained.

"Two months ago, the regulator came to us and said that our finance submission was out of line with our risk submission. This caused us to divert key resources from our team for almost two months to trawl through the differences and the contents of the systems that produce the reports to explain them. The context of the reports had been lost, making the job much harder. The contexts define the outputs of the reports, and the requirements on data in finance are different to the requirements in risk. Therefore, you expect the numbers to be different. It would be good to have this information to hand so that we can quickly explain the gaps," Brian explained.

"That makes sense; what are the numbers predominantly reporting?" Jennifer asked.

"The numbers are reporting the risk exposure and profitability by business line. We split the businesses across retail, corporate, and markets, and then within each of these they are split by product line. For retail it is mortgages, bank accounts, loans, cards, etc., and for markets it is rates, credit, foreign exchange, equities, commodities, etc. To produce most of the risk or P&L reports, we need to aggregate calculations based on these businesses together. Some reports are based on the customer, other reports are based on the products and positions. It is important for us to have this information to hand with the applied model so that it can be combined to be able to answer the questions that we have," Brian explained.

"Would it be possible to see the reports that you need to produce?" Jennifer understood what Brian was explaining very well; however, she knew that she needed to see the data firsthand and therefore the reports themselves.

"Yes, I can email the team to grant you access to our shared drive, where they are stored," Brian said.

"I will look at the reports, as this is always a good starting point. I would guess, though, that if we just produced these reports with nothing else, then nobody would use them?" Jennifer enquired to tease out more of how the business were using the data.

"I am not sure what you mean. We always look to use the systems that we specify," Brian said.

Jennifer was being deliberately challenging to be able to make a really important point. "I am guessing if we produced a system that would provide your teams with exactly the layout of the reports you already produce, the first thing that would happen is that you would want to extract the data that produced the numbers?" she enquired.

"We have to sign off the numbers to be sure that we trust them and reconcile them back to a trusted source," Brian said.

Jennifer realised it was time to explain. "What I have found is that a data system is not defined by the pretty formatted reports that are generated; it is defined by the way that the users can interact and get comfortable with the data in the system. People do not like it when the answer is produced, and they are asked to trust it. There is a whole lot of interaction with the data and understanding of the numbers that needs to happen before people will trust a system. Therefore, there is little usage of the systems that have been specified to date, which is highlighted by some stats that I have seen. If we do not design the system to be used in the way that people want to use the system, it will not be used!

"I reviewed the business requirements documents (BRDs) that have been produced to date, and they did not involve human interaction—they are full of end reports and formulas as well as sources of data. I need to change the way that these are being produced so that we can understand the system that your team needs. We will then have factored in their interactions into the design and built tools to enable them to achieve their jobs more efficiently," Jennifer explained.

"How do you propose to do that?" Brian enquired with some concern to the additional work this could generate.

"There is a process for specifications that I have used over the years that has enabled me to help define the parts that BRDs miss. I call it the clear SCOPE process where a vision of the system is established through the following:

Storyboards—How will the users use the system?
Content—What is the content required to satisfy the requirement?
Output—What needs to be output from the system—for example, reports, feeds, etc.—to be able to satisfy the requirement?
Process—What is the process that the data goes through for it to be able to produce the correct key performance indicators (KPIs) and metrics?
Easiness—How easy is it to produce the requirement based on the information provided?

"There is important content in the BRDs that maps onto this structure, but there is not enough information to articulate what is really needed! My plan is to work with Ian Cole and to make sure that the additional information is being captured in the process. The additional information will enable us to fully understand the full process that the teams go through; it also includes standard information in a more consumable format, which will help us build a system organised to produce results quickly and effectively as requirements change. The final part of the SCOPE process is for us to work together as a sponsorship team to establish the priority of items on the list. In my experience, there are some requirements that, on the outset, look and sound easy but are either incredibly complicated to implement or they require huge amounts of storage or processing power to calculate," Jennifer explained.

"So, to summarise, you want to increase the conversations with the user team to improve communication. This will put greater strain on my already busy resources. They are already having to work long hours to produce the reporting now—they are not going to be happy at spending more time," Brian summarised his understanding.

"The best way to look at what I am saying is that the investment in time on the correct activities will give you systems that users can use and will need less testing. It will enable you to remove the ecosystem from around the outside of the existing tools that you have built up over time. The plan will be to define the target vision and then instrument the pipeline so that we know from the data what is possible and what is not. We would then document the data correctly to make sure that it stays consistent with the implementation.

"Next, we would engineer a platform so that we can extend it with new requirements over time and not have to reengineer. This will give us the capability to engineer changing requirements rapidly and effectively, without the need for large amounts of rework.

"Finally, our job as a management team would be for the governance and control around the platform and solution to make sure that it remains on track towards the target and contains the quality that people want to use. This takes a degree of discipline, which, if we get the solution right, then we should be able to encapsulate it within the work that the teams already do," Jennifer said to sum up the process that she had followed many times.

"How do you propose to capture and maintain all of this data? All of our existing efforts have taken huge amounts of work and effort to build dictionaries and assign roles, and nobody has really felt that it has enhanced their job," Brian explained.

"I know, it is a common problem with traditional approaches. The problem is that they are not built into someone's tasks, so they feel like they are an additional effort. What you find is that people are doing the work required already in their jobs to document and understand metrics and data and to validate results and check for data quality. The problem is that they are not captured in the right place or captured at all. If we build the system to capture the information and logic as part of their everyday procedures, then it should happen as part of the overall process," Jennifer explained.

"You say we capture this information; where do we capture it?" Brian asked.

"The teams that you have on the business side that take the data from the database and then cleanse it in spreadsheets and other end user tools (EUCs) that contain cleansing rules, or they are manually adjusting data. They also know what the right answer is, since they are having to produce it on a monthly or quarterly basis. The problem is the logic that they are applying is locked up in their heads or in the EUCs and not systemised. The key to building a reliable data system is to capture that effort and work it into the data and metadata so that over time it becomes automated," Jennifer explained.

"That is a lot of work; some of the people have been doing this for years!" Brian exclaimed, realising the size of the challenge.

"You are right, it is a lot of work. I will not pretend this is going to be easy or be done overnight. The key to it is to set up the processes to start the journey so that we are moving forwards. Every iteration then takes us closer to the target and frees up time to be able to put more effort into moving forwards. Over time the efforts start to accumulate, and the productivity of the teams improves. This provides motivation to move forwards faster with more efficiency. To make sure that we are moving forwards we need to instrument the data pipeline from front to back to measure the improvements. Again, this is huge task, but the purpose is to start small and gain some wins and then allow this to grow outwards," Jennifer explained.

"OK, so this sounds sensible. What are the next steps, and how do we make sure that this is tracking in the right direction?" Brian asked.

"Firstly, I need to assess where the project, architecture, people, and processes are. This will take a couple of weeks of meeting with key individuals and starting to move them in the correct direction. I then suggest that we pick an area and start to move it forwards, as described, to enable us to put the frameworks in place that can be repeated over time across the rest of the business. As time permits, we move more streams into this process to move them forwards," Jennifer explained.

"Which area do you suggest is the area to focus on to start this approach with?" Brian asked.

"I would suggest the best area is the one that is most receptive to moving forwards and changing approach. I would expect it is the one that has a well-defined use case and they are trying to achieve a specific outcome. There needs to be motivation to want to achieve a goal. Looking at the work that is on the backlog, the most pressing requirements looks to be the "Aspen" project. It is relatively new, and, therefore, we can get in on the ground and have the most influence. Many of the other projects are looking to feed off this, so it will give us the ideal seed project to start on," Jennifer said.

"I agree, the Aspen project is a key delivery for us this year. It is putting demands on my team that are outside their day-to-day operations. The regulator has provided a specification for what they want from us, but the templates are complex and not particularly well thought through. For example, they have asked for P&L data to be provided alongside risk data. I understand what they are trying to achieve, but the way the data lines up is not really the way that we operate. It is going to take a whole lot of work to align the data.

"The templates also ask for information to be presented rolled up by customer segment and business line; however, the segments they have provided do not match the logical segments that we would use. In addition to this, the numbers that they are asking for are quite different to the numbers that we have in our existing risk processes. The team have run analysis, and they have worked out a plan to implement the calculations, but it is a lot of data to generate—more than we are used to—and they are having issues in getting results out.

"Our aim is to be able to get the models to generate these types of problems and then to store them in a single location that people can pull the information from to satisfy the regulatory requirement. The challenge is that every time we try to do this, we end up with completely different sets of segments, calculations, and populations. This has forced us to build point solutions for each regulation that cannot be reused," Brian explained.

"That does sound like the right target for us to be working on." Jennifer thought through the problem described. It was complex but could be simplified considerably with the right approach. She had worked on similar projects, and the challenge lined up nicely with what she suspected was one of the key issues. It would come down to the organisation of the data and how it was being treated and managed. She needed to be sure that there were no expectation gaps between Brian's thinking and what could be achieved; she also needed to make sure that there were no requirements around the corner that would catch the team off guard and cause the momentum to be lost.

"I looked at the BRD for the Aspen project last night. The specification is largely asking for exposures in the form of sensitivities, and they are comparing this to the P&L numbers due to changes in the market. The grids seem to be aggregating the data by product and geography, with different measures across the top. You mentioned just now that they do not line up to your operational numbers. What are the differences between the op numbers and these reports?" Jennifer asked.

"The numbers in these reports represent sensitivities and KPIs that we do not normally monitor. It is not typically how the business works. We are going to have to create a whole new set of numbers to flow through the system. That is not unusual—the challenge with the methodology is that they have asked to classify the trades and securities using brand new classifications. The countries are rolled up differently to normal, and the rules for the sectors are different to the rules we have for our internal sectors.

"The flags do not exist in Security Store for this; to change them is a huge amount of work and has impact on all the systems downstream of Security Store. Due to the increased payload, we are having issues mapping the classifications and flowing them through the system to get them into the reporting system. Changes are taking forever to run through and to check them at the far end in the reports," Brian said.

Jennifer was aware of the issue with the data not lining up but was unsure why it had created such a challenge for the project. "OK, that sounds like we need to look at the flow of information through the system. I have set up a meeting with Justin Parkins to go through the current implementation as soon as I understand the requirements and the underlying data flows. Moving on, what is the ambition for the system after satisfying this requirement?" she asked.

"Ideally, we want to make this system a framework that will enable us to run all of the different regulatory reporting through. The previous implementations of the reports have been done as point solutions that are costing a lot of headcount to maintain. It would be good if they could all flow through consistently so that I can build economies of scale," Brian explained.

"The other issue is that previous implementations seem to require many applications built by my team to make them work for us. This needs to be cleaned up so that we can focus my team on managing the controls rather than being the controls and processes," he added.

"That makes sense, and I know how to address a number of these issues. In the next phase of the system, what are likely to be the analysis and exposures that you will be addressing?" Jennifer asked.

Brian took a moment to think. "We need to look at the exposures and risks on a customer basis to monitor our exposures to individual entities and their parents. This would help us to enable better credit and counterparty risk and P&L. Currently this is in a completely different system, and the two do not agree with each other. This is denting the confidence in the organisation that we know what we are doing and what we are exposed to. We seem to spend more time in the risk committees arguing about the numbers presented rather than discussing how we should be managing the risks. This then spawns more work to be able to explain the differences to management, who want to be sure they are acting on real data," Brian explained.

"OK, in summary, the solution needs to include a single version of the truth that is used as the foundation for the reporting that gets produced. This needs to be traceable and of high quality to start to gain back the confidence of the risk committees and the risk management. You are then looking to add in a counterparty analysis capability," Jennifer summarised.

"Yes, correct, and it also needs to be timely for current requirements and be dynamic so that future requirements extend the framework and are easy to implement. We should not be creating a completely different flow for every new requirement. Having said that, we should not be completely rewriting the data flow every time that we are asked for something new," Brian said.

"OK, that makes a lot of sense and is consistent with my own philosophy. Anything else that you think needs to be included?" Jennifer asked.

"The other key factor is that we need to get the teams using the system to cut down on the amount of manual work that we are having to do. The team need to be using the system as the current manual processes present a risk to the production of official numbers. There needs to be a lot more governance and control around what we are doing and far fewer manual steps," Brian said.

"I would counter that slightly, as my experience is that the manual steps that your team are undertaking are essential to the production of quality numbers. The key thing we need to do is encapsulate the steps that they take within a controlled system rather than in manual spreadsheets and emails. Would that make sense to you?" Jennifer asked.

"Yes, it would. A lot of what they are doing is to cleanse the data from upstream and to make it line up to the reporting requirements. The ideal would be to fix issues upstream so that it flows through correctly, but this is not feasible in the timelines of the reports and submissions. We therefore need to cleanse downstream to get them out," Brian explained.

"I am guessing there are so many of these cleanses that the fixes rarely find their way back to the upstream systems, and therefore the same task has to be repeated for the next iteration?" Jennifer asked.

"Yes, in part, we try to fix the obvious issues, but many have lots of dependencies, which prevent us from addressing them," Brian said.

"OK, I know a number of ways to make this work more efficiently within the system. We can look to implement these within Aspen and then extend in the future. I will take this as a requirement to move things forwards," Jennifer said scribbling down another point in her notebook.

Jennifer thought that for this meeting she had captured enough and understood Brian's vision, which would enable her to move forwards. It was now worth summarising the points that they had discussed. "Brian, in summary:

- Project Aspen makes the most sense to focus on.
- We need to look at its implementation through reviewing the requirements to make sure that it captures what is needed operationally as well as what is needed physically to make sure that people use the system.
- We need to look at ways to encapsulate the data quality information into the flow rather than as an add-on at the end.

- The iterations need to speed up to improve the momentum in the project.
- The reports do not represent a standard way that we monitor risk internally, so we need a quick way to store the information in a standard way but report out specifically for each business requirement.
- We need to build Aspen as a framework that we can then repeat across the other projects in the department and across the organisation.
- The framework needs to be created to be extensible so that new requirements can be incorporated without completely rewriting the solution.
- The solution needs to extend into counterparty / credit risk after doing the risk and P&L reports.
- There needs to be a way to reconcile numbers between P&L and risk to report each as a known basis and be able to map between them.
- The governance of the system needs to be integrated into the business process rather than as an add-on to the system that becomes expensive to maintain.
- We will need separate parts of the project that can be run in an agile way to those that cannot so that we can work more effectively and build project momentum.

"I will write up minutes of this so that we can document the vision for Aspen and beyond. We can use it as a target for us to move towards so that it guides our approach," Jennifer said.

"Can we move onto housekeeping?" she asked.

Brian was satisfied with the summary of the points Jennifer had recounted. "Yes, please."

"Are you OK if I set up a monthly meeting in the diary between us to discuss progress and to work through the next steps that we are taking? I will also join the monthly steering meeting with the key stakeholders and yourself to be able to guide the project in the direction that we need it to go. I will be setting up specific meetings around the scope definition process over the coming weeks to fill in the gaps for the project to enable us to move forwards more effectively. I will also look to put together a communication pack after my assessment that goes through what we need to do for us to be able to move the vision forward more efficiently. Anything else that you think that we need?" Jennifer asked.

"I will need a project plan for the end delivery to the regulator soon so that we can start planning for how we can meet this deadline. There is a lot riding on this, and I need to be able to reassure senior management that we are on track and able to meet deadlines," Brian said.

"OK, I will make that part of the output of the assessment so that we can manage that effectively. Thank you for your time, Brian, I look forward to moving this vision forwards with you," Jennifer said.

"Thank you, Jennifer, we have our work cut out to be able to make these changes quickly and effectively. I want to stay on top of things. If you come across issues, please do not hesitate to contact me," Brian said.

"I will, and I look forward to working with you going forwards," said Jennifer.

Jennifer walked out of the meeting feeling that they had made some good progress. She felt the tension that existed in Brian, who was desperate to make something work to take the pressure off his team. The reality was that the solutions were taking too long, and the team were not able to use the IT-led solutions to their full potential. Jennifer knew she had a honeymoon period, but she needed to show deliveries and some form of step change in the process for her to win over a low-confidence business group.

The first thing to address was to get the requirements better defined in terms of real information. The SCOPE process would give them a much better articulation of what was needed for the Aspen project. The information that had been gained from meeting with Brian would add flesh to the bones of the BRDs. There would need to be more work done on the BRD process to provide artefacts that they could work reliably from. Her next meeting would be to catch up with Ian Cole so they could review the approach.

"First things first," she thought to herself. It was important to play back her notes and summary of the meeting to Brian. It was important that they were on the same page moving forwards as she would need his support to drive things the way she knew they needed to go. The trick to data projects lay between the collaboration of business, IT, and control functions. The business owned the data and were the subject matter experts (SMEs) when it came to understanding how to calculate the numbers and present them. IT were the facilitators of the official pipelines and tools. All of it needed to be governed in a way that enabled responsible use of the data and the output.

Jennifer spent the next part of the day writing up her notes in her office. She also wanted to prepare for the meeting with her new team that Mark had organised. Mark had booked the large conference room and invited the teams that would now be under Jennifer's lead. Mark was efficient at running these meetings, and they were organised around a typical schedule.

First there would be an explanation of the business landscape, then the requirement to align to this challenge, and then the introduction of the new structure. Finally, introducing Jennifer and a Q&A session. From talking to her team, Jennifer realised that many of the key individuals knew what was coming, and many were happy of the chance of wider responsibilities. She knew there would be others who would be harder to convince. Once this meeting was over, then she could really start to work with the individuals in leadership positions in her team.

The meeting ran as expected. Mark held the audience with his delivery, and then Jennifer said a few words to explain how much she was looking forward to the opportunity and the challenges ahead.

The announcement would allow Jennifer to start moving ahead with getting her arms around the Aspen project and setting up meetings with key managers in her team.

First up was meeting with Ian Cole, where she hoped to understand more about the business requirements documents and more about the challenges of sitting between the business needs and the IT delivery. She scheduled the meeting for early the following morning and made sure she hard copies of the Aspen BRD to hand.

It was getting late, and it had been quite an intense day. It was time to head home and get some rest before the next day.

Closing Questions

To improve your data and analytics programmes, you need to make sure there is a well-defined shared vision. Here are some questions that need to be answered:

- For your data and analytics programmes, do all stakeholders have a shared vision on what you are trying to achieve?
- Is this vision defined in a way to act as a compass setting for the overall initiative?
- Have you got clear sponsorship defined with someone who is passionate about the outcome of the initiative?
- Is the vision defining the mountain range or the immediate peak in front of you?
- Do you have a relationship with your business where there is enough trust to discuss the mountain range?

Chapter 2

Setting the Target

Key Concepts

A business requirements document (BRD) is often used in organisations to define the requirements for a data and analytics solution—either this or basic use cases and mock-ups of outputs and calculations. The problem with this approach is that the requirement is defined without the people and process included. To complete the story, the users who are consuming the output of this report need to be comfortable that the data within it is telling them the right thing. Possibly their job or the outcome of a business decision will be determined by the data that is presented. On many occasions users extract data into desktop tools from the systems provided by IT. The desktop tools are getting more sophisticated and enable users to cleanse, amend, group, categorise, and manipulate the information to be sure of its origins and accuracy.

The goal of DataOps is to build systems that users can do their cleansing, grouping, and business rules within, helping the organisation move forward in a more collaborative and productive way. By following this approach, one of our consulting teams was able to deliver a solution in eight weeks, where the existing team had been struggling with it for six months. I attribute this to the ability to get the focus of all the stakeholders on the problem and to build a complete solution. Kinaesis have developed the clear SCOPE definition process for capturing the right level of information for a project, and we see this as critically important to our success.

J ENNIFER HAD booked the meeting with Ian for early morning, and she had blocked out most of the morning to review the existing requirements process. She wanted to learn more about Ian and the team and the challenges that they faced. It was clear there was a disconnect between the business and IT, but the root cause would be more difficult to diagnose than just the symptoms that were visible.

Ian Cole was an experienced hand and had worked on several of the large requirements analysis tasks for the big finance system projects. He had a good rapport with the business and was able to form good working relationships to help him build trust. His team was more junior, and they needed some structure around their analysis activities. They followed the standard BRD process, which had been tried and tested on many of the operational system builds.

Ian was first to the meeting room and had taken a seat by the window when Jennifer arrived.

"Hello Ian, I hope you are well," Jennifer came in cheerfully and warmly, and pulled up a chair at the end of the table adjacent to Ian.

"Hello Jennifer, congratulations on your promotion."

"Thank you," Jennifer responded. "It is a big step up, and there are lots of new pressures with the role, but I hope we can make lots of progress with our projects."

"I imagine there is a lot of pressure across the whole organisation, with all eyes focusing on the Aspen project," Ian said.

"Yes, but from what I have seen, it is still achievable. I called this meeting to go through the requirements process and to review the existing artefacts and the process that we are following currently. I was then wanting to work with yourself to talk through some of the challenges and to explore some opportunities to improve the process. Is that OK with you?" Jennifer asked.

"Yes, happy to work through things, and we need to look at how to speed delivery up. As it stands, we are not in position to achieve our outcomes," Ian stated.

Jennifer and Ian then worked through each of the projects and the business requirements documents, going through the background and the underlying requirements and sources of the information gathered. It was a good way to build a connection before Jennifer wanted to start to talk about how they could move things forwards.

"How have things been going with yourself?" Jennifer asked.

"Where do I start? Firstly, we have produced all the current batch of business requirements for the targeted projects that we have just reviewed. Project Aspen has been fully specified. It was a complex piece of analysis, the risk calculations were different to the ones we are used to, and the layout of the outputs are not using the same codes that we are used to. We have provided the development teams with the specifications on time to review. We have produced an extensive mapping document showing them the business logic for producing all the fields on the report," Ian said.

"Sounds like it is going well. What is the feedback from the development team?" Jennifer asked.

Ian slightly flinched. "Well, they have had a look and they have provided quite a lot of feedback."

"What sort of feedback?" Jennifer asked.

"Well, they went through the logic and mentioned that it is difficult for them to replicate. There is a lot of data, and the logic was complicated and would take lots of processing," Ian said.

"What do you think?" Jennifer asked.

"The logic is the logic. The business asked for what they needed. It is not as if they had a choice, as they are bound by the regulator, so it is hard for me to be able to adjust the information that we write down," Ian said.

"Did the specification consist of a calculation part and a post-calculation part, for formatting and aggregation?" Jennifer asked.

"Yes, it was really complicated; some of the classifications of securities changed from what we are used to, so we had to feed these through from the calculation engine for them to be used in the reports," Ian said.

"It does sound difficult," Jennifer said, trying to empathise with Ian.

"The calculation engine was the most logical place to put the classifications, as the security information originates in the Security Store system," Ian continued. "The second complexity came with the country groupings; again, we put them into the calculation engine to feed them through," Ian said.

"How is the testing going of the initial runs?" Jennifer asked.

"It is difficult; it is taking ages to get the results out of the calculation engine and into the users' hands. We got the test data through the system last week, and a lot of the classifications were wrong. We sent the new file to the calculation team ready for a new run. They expect it to be next week to get this to run through the calculation engines again," Ian said.

He continued. "I was told that the IT team are struggling with the capacity of the system, so each run seems to be taking an age to get through to the reporting system. We cannot do much until they can get the information through correctly. We have been spending a lot of our time trying to appease the users, who are frustrated at the speed of change," Ian mentioned.

"OK, how much of the calculations rely on the numbers that are in the sectors and the country groupings?" Jennifer asked.

Ian thought for a minute. "The calculations are not dependent on the country groupings at all; why do you ask?"

Jennifer wanted Ian to start to think things through for himself, so she was allowing his thoughts to unfold. "It seems unusual to me why you would add the country groupings and the securities at the start of the data pipeline. Any changes to them would always take weeks to make and test," Jennifer challenged.

"We spoke to the users, and this was the most convenient place to put them. They interact with the setting of the calculations, so at that point they would be able to set up the sectors and countries within the front end!" Ian said.

"It makes sense for convenience, but it has created a huge dependency on changing of the data downstream," Jennifer persisted.

"Yes, but how else could we have done it?" Ian was getting a little defensive, as it was starting to dawn on him that maybe by taking the easy route up front it was costing the project further down the line.

Jennifer, sensing his defensive nature, wanted to reassure Ian but also to make sure that he would think through the problem in front of him. "Where on the pipeline from calculation through to reporting does the dependency for the groupings and the sectors first appear?" Jennifer asked.

"We would want to store the sectors in the risk store, so I guess that would be the first place that we would want them to exist," Ian said.

"Yes, and across reporting in the enterprise, how many processes are impacted by these sectors and groupings?" Jennifer asked.

Ian took a moment to think. "These sectors and groupings are specific to this requirement only."

"OK, so should these be stored as part of the overall model or as part of the reporting for this submission?" Jennifer asked.

"Probably part of the reporting for this submission," Ian said.

"When you add the data to the calculated data at the beginning of the pipeline, how much data does that add to each of the risk results?" Jennifer asked.

"The groupings are about fifty characters long, and the sectors about the same. Considering the codes and the timestamps, then probably about one hundred bytes for each," Ian said.

"OK, and how many risk results are you expecting?" Jennifer asked.

"We have one million active positions on the books that we are calculating risk for, and there are over three hundred metrics that we need to calculate for this submission," Ian said.

"So, doing the rough math's, we have one million positions, multiplied by three hundred metrics, multiplied by two hundred bytes. So that represents roughly sixty gigabytes of extra data per risk run for these classifications," Jennifer calculated, doing the math's approximately in her head.

"Yes, I guess it does. We were told that with Big Data, size does not matter because storage is cheap," Ian mentioned.

"In my view, that is not the point of Big Data. Storing information that you do not physically need to store and relating it to information that you know may change over time is one of the big issues. To illustrate this, think of this scenario," Jennifer said thinking through an example she had sadly seen in the past.

"We are running the risk process daily for a whole year. The sectors are moving around, and the users are changing what they need for reporting rapidly. We have stored roughly two hundred and sixty times sixty gigabytes of extra data on disk, linked to the risk runs. This now represents fourteen terabytes of extra information stored in Big Data. We now are asked to run a trend over the historical data to be able to show people how our risk position has changed over time. The person asks that for the trend we use the sector that is current right now on the risk results and to project it backwards. How would we do this?" Jennifer asked.

Ian thought through the problem. "We would need to go through the back history of the data and set the sector to the current sector and then report out the data as required," he said.

"Typically, Big Data systems are read and write systems, and update performance tends to be poor. Even so, if we were to do this and the following day the person changes their mind and says that the sector from last month is more reliable and we should use that one for the reporting, do we go in and change the sector all over again?" Jennifer asked again.

"No, that would be crazy. It would take a long time to keep doing this," Ian stated.

"OK, so given this, then how would you think you should store the data in the system?" Jennifer was needing to hammer the point home that the specification of the data mapping and requirements needed to take into consideration the flow of data through the system, the scope, and the volatility of the variables. If Ian understood the importance of this, then he would be able to guide and explain this to his team. It would also enable her to change the approach and the data that they capture going forwards so that they could start to speed up the iterations.

Ian took a little longer to answer this time as he thought through the shape of the data in the systems. "If we do not add the data at the start, then we would have to add it towards the reporting end of the system. We could add it close to these regulatory reports, and then it would be specific to these reports," Ian said looking slightly relieved.

"Yes, it would then also mean that a change to the classifications would only require us to reprocess the reports. It normally takes a couple of minutes to preprocess the reports, hence we would be able to iterate with the solution much quicker, and fixing the classifications can happen without it impacting the resources of the calculators and the storage in the risk store," Jennifer said.

Ian was starting to think through the implications of moving the information closer to the users and how it would make his job easier.

"So, would it be a big change to add the management of the classifications to the reporting layer?" Jennifer enquired.

"Probably not systemwise," Ian thought. "We could join the classifications to risk just before it is presented back to the users. It would be a change to the procedures for the users though, which they are not aware of, and they do not have a tool outside of the risk calculator for maintaining these mappings. We would have to build them a new tool to maintain the mappings that we do not have yet," Ian said.

"In order to allow the projects to move forwards more rapidly, could we allow the users to maintain the mappings manually and then add them into the pipeline near the reports?" Jennifer asked. "We could then add to the backlog a tool that manages them more formally in later iterations once the deadline for producing the regulatory report has passed," Jennifer said.

"Yes, I do not see why not. The users tend to build up mappings offline to be able to run checks and to make amendments to the reporting before it is submitted. We have never been able to create perfectly clean reports directly through the system that can be submitted. The regulatory reporting solution is not flexible enough for them to be able to cleanse all the data quality issues in time for the submission. This would mean that they need to produce a mapping to feed in," Ian explained.

Jennifer was pleased with the speed of Ian's thinking on the issues and his response to seeing the opportunity in her suggestion. She sensed he was as frustrated with the speed of change as anyone, and he was keen for them to produce a solution that could help move the project forwards. Jennifer needed him to start to look at the requirements process in a new way, and in her experience, the best way to achieve this was to provide input that would enable people to see the benefits of looking at things differently. Once they saw the benefits, then they would open and see other things that could be done differently to improve things. Now that she had achieved the initial acceptance, it was going to be easier to explain the bigger picture.

"Ian, in summary, what we have just worked through is the mapping process that they can apply at the end of the pipeline that empowers them to cleanse the data and rerun the reporting. This will enable them to run iterations of the data mapping much quicker, and not only that, they will bring the offline mappings that they currently do in spreadsheets and enter them into the system. The key for us speeding up the rate of iterations is going to be differentiating the actual logical workflow from the logical system workflow; we then need to encompass the working practices of the users into the organisation of the data pipeline.

"On previous projects that I have led and been involved with, we worked on a process called SCOPE. This enabled us to map out the business process through **S**toryboards, categorise the **C**ontent, define the **O**utput, establish the data **P**rocesses, and consider the **E**xpense of making the change. I would like to move to this system in the Aspen project to enable us to move forwards more effectively. Many of the steps in it are aligned to what you currently do with the bank standard BRD process, but there are additional steps that will help to clarify the requirements in a way that enables us to keep the project moving forwards in an agile way.

"In my experience, data projects have a real pull towards a waterfall delivery process with heavy dependencies forcing you down this road. The trick is to design the projects so that they can maintain agility. Moving the report mappings to the end of the data pipeline is one of the many ways to empower the teams in a controlled way that then enables the data to be managed by the people on the project centrally, rather than outside of the system where control is lost," Jennifer said.

"OK, but we are halfway through the project. It is going to be difficult to employ a whole new approach right now!" Ian was looking concerned that a change of course could completely take them off their timeline.

"You are right," Jennifer reassured him. "We need to introduce the new methodology in a way to improve the parts of the existing project as much as we can whilst maintaining momentum. We can do this by introducing quick wins like the one above to build momentum and hold back disruptive changes in the first instance. Over the course of time the methods can be expanded into a more structured approach."

Ian was thinking this through. "So, what are the changes that you think we can introduce right now?"

"Firstly, we need to Storyboard the process and draw up how numbers get into the end reports. We will need to have conversations with the users to document the output of the reports and then categorise the content by understanding a little about the sources of the information driving the reports. This will not take too long, because there is a fair amount of the information captured already—we just need to categorise it more effectively. Over time it will take less time because we will start to build up a metadata store that contains all the information to help accelerate the process. By Storyboarding and supporting the users' processes, we should be able to put the data in the hands of the users to help them run the reporting and provide us with the knowledge of what they do to cleanse the reports. By working together on this with the users, we can hopefully start to bridge the gap between their expectations and what is possible. This should in turn help out the IT teams to take some of the pressure off," Jennifer explained.

"The other thing that we can do straight away is to look at the content and output formats and to help us model the processes," Jennifer added.

Ian looked a little puzzled on this. He was thinking if we have Storyboarded the users' activities, then surely this represented the processes. "What do mean by the processes?" he asked.

"I mean the data processes at the lowest level. When you look at the output and the content, there are two things that we need to work out:

- We need to work out the day in the life of the data. It is likely that the timing of the information from one feed could be out of synch with the data from another feed. It could also mean that the data is not available in the timeliness that the business requires the data in. Having conversations about this before implementation and resolving the issues in the data timing is key.
- The second part of the puzzle is the way that the data needs to be represented to support what the users need in the process of producing the numbers. For instance, take positions—they are the sum of the transactions that have gone before. If I buy one hundred bonds, and then sell fifty, my position is fifty bonds. However, the requirement may specify that although the position exists, the information required is for transactions to be able to support the reporting output. It is important that we understand this before we provide specifications or requirements to the IT teams, as it completely changes the scale of the data that we need. This is hugely important because we get the feed of positions and transactions from other teams who have a full workload, and it takes them a long time to produce new feeds, which could severely impact our timelines," Jennifer explained.

"This sounds like quite a lot of information and skills that we do not currently have on the team to make these kinds of decisions in the specifications. How do you think we can approach this to be able to make the changes that we need to?" Ian was starting to be concerned with the amount of work he was seeing in front of him. It was not clear where he would fit this in.

It was key that Jennifer did not overwhelm him, but she still needed him to make the necessary changes if the projects were going to be successful. She thought through Ian's skills and wanted to play to his strengths and support him through the changes. "Are you comfortable with the Storyboarding process?" she asked.

"What would this contain?" he asked.

"Well, it involves looking at the user processes that happen from the front to back to produce reliable numbers in the reports," she answered.

"Yes, we work closely with the users, so we know what they are doing. It is fairly easy for me to document this so that we can produce the reporting," Ian said confidently, happy that he had a good understanding of the business.

"It is important that you capture all of the steps that they take through the IT processes and the user processes after they have extracted the information," Jennifer added.

"Yes, I think I know it reasonably well, but I will need to meet with a few of the key users to clarify," Ian said.

"OK, so if we start here then when you are documenting this, I would like you to work with the users to produce a specification of the data that they need to carry out the Storyboard activities within the flow. This could be a reconciliation source, analytics set, or just the level of grain / drill down they require. If you add that to the data mapping and explain the process that is involved, then the next stages we can work together on. There is one of my team members, Dan Churchill, who has worked with me on previous projects, who will be able to guide you on the next two processes. If I team you together for this one, he can show your team what to do this time around, and then next time around he can look to review what has been done," Jennifer explained.

"When we meet the users to map the end-to-end process, what should we be capturing?" Ian asked.

"If you start with the output that is required to be produced from this project, there is likely to be several different phases.

1. Sign off phase—This will normally be for large global submissions organised in a hierarchy to break the work down. It could be by business line, or product line, or a combination of both, based around systems of record.

2. Adjustment phase—There will be a process at the end representing the fine tuning of the reports. At this stage it will be last-minute adjustments to numbers to bring them in line with the correct numbers. We need a definition of what is being adjusted and where and when and by who.

3. Reconciliation phase—This could, and should, happen at multiple stages in the process of producing results. There will be a set of metrics and rules and potentially other sources that need to be identified here.

4. Formatting phase—This is where the raw numbers are mapped onto the aggregate numbers, and then the mappings are adjusted and amended to get them to come out correctly.

5. Cleansing stage—This is where the data is examined and checked and then regenerated as required.

6. Analysis phase—In most of the above, the users will want to be able to understand a high-level number and then drill down into what it consists of and check underlying numbers. This will normally be in conjunction to some threshold checks that need to be done. It will normally involve comparisons to previous numbers.

"In each of these phases, the users will have a certain set of content they need. The purpose of the Storyboarding process is to work through this data and capture it in a template. What you capture needs to be specific—for example, when you see country in a report you need to understand which country this is." Jennifer explained.

"I am not sure I understand—what you mean by which country this is?" Ian asked.

"Well, country is a static dataset. There are 197 countries in the world; however, when we report, we are identifying the country of an entity, generally. For example, country of the Customer, country of the Banks entity, country of the security, etc. When the team capture the content, they need to capture this information," Jennifer explained.

"That makes sense. We do that, but I am not sure we are explicit in the capture," Ian said.

"The second thing that you need to capture is the source of the field. There will be a current actual source that is being used, or is required, and this can be compared against the preferred source," Jennifer continued.

"What is the preferred source?" Ian asked.

"The preferred source is not something that we formally capture at the moment, but we will be building this up as a set of information that we capture in the metadata," Jennifer said.

"That does not sound like too much on top of what we currently do. The users currently work with a series of spreadsheets and access databases to carry out these processes. We can ask them to provide these to us, and then we can capture the information within these," Ian said.

"Is there a format that you want to capture the data in?" he asked.

"To be fair to the existing process, the mapping sheets already in the specification capture a lot of this information. We should be able to add some additional columns to these. We will then extend the mappings to include the new Storyboard content." Jennifer said.

"If you show me after the meeting, I can get the team onto it as soon as today," Ian said.

Ian was enthusiastic about his task, and given that he was waiting on some test results, it would give him and his team a focus for the next few days. Jennifer was conscious of not getting too excited just yet; the changes were always greeted with enthusiasm at the start, but there was a way to go before the full benefit and approach would be accepted. The meeting had reached a logical conclusion, and there was enough to be getting on with capturing the Storyboards and the content. They walked out of the meeting room together and headed to their desks.

Jennifer set up a one-to-one with Ian to make sure she could provide the input and advice he would need. When she got back to her desk, she wrote a quick note to Brian Catts to make him aware of Ian's new plan. It was going to take up a little more of the users' time, and she needed to pre-warn Brian to manage his team. Her next task was to talk to Dan Churchill, who had been working with Jennifer for the last three years building out SCOPE documents. She would need his help in guiding Ian's team to produce the required output. Dan was very capable, but also a good mentor and good with people.

Jennifer's next task was to establish where they were with the architecture function. The existing architecture would have to evolve to enable it to be more flexible for new requirements to keep up with user demand. This would take time, but there would be enough small wins to be able to make progress and start to change the velocity.

Jennifer spent the rest of the day helping Ian set up the new mapping templates. Ian and his team made the amendments and then wrote down instructions on what to fill in. The team picked up the task quickly and were ready to go and collect the information by the end of the day. Tomorrow she would be working with Justin Parkins to understand more about the challenges of the IT development teams.

Closing Questions

When building a requirements definition for a data and analytics project or user story, it needs to include all the elements required. Here are some questions to get you thinking:

- Does your requirements definition just include the reports and calculations?
- Are you assuming a data warehouse and BI tool when collecting requirements?
- Do you capture the right data and information in the requirements process?
- Do you thoroughly understand how the users use the data in their business process, or how they should use the data?
- Do you have confidence in the completeness of the solution that you are building that the users will not need to work outside of the platform?

Chapter 3

Understanding the Platform

Key Concepts

Heroes exist; they put themselves out for a cause, often working all hours to solve problems and help things to move smoothly. However, sometimes this culture highlights underlying flaws in an approach. By using clever design and thinking in the first place, then maybe there is no need for heroics. This is what DataOps is about. One of the key challenges with data is that it is constantly flowing and changing. Therefore, a set of patterns needs to be established to "expect the unexpected" and to enable the custodians of the system to deal with issues efficiently and effectively.

One of these key patterns is monitoring at all stages of the data pipeline and building in continuous improvement. This includes improvement in the monitoring and improvement in the diagnosis tools, as well as improvement in the ability to respond to changing requirements and needs. Often we expect a single tool to solve today's challenges and those of tomorrow and to be all things to all men. This has been the case with Big Data, where the hype is huge, and everyone tries to implement solutions using the technology without fully understanding what it was built for and how it maps onto the business requirement. The answer is not about expecting technology to be the silver bullet. The answer is the correct definition of a challenge and then fitting the right architecture and technology to solve it, building in flexibility to meet the requirements today but also in the future.

THE MEETING with Justin was set up for the following morning. Jennifer had spent much of the previous evening reading the documentation on the existing architecture. This included the cost justification for the data lake and the other technology selections in the solution stack. She went back over her notes from the meeting with Mark Denby.

The new morning was sunny and bright as Jennifer walked from the tube station to the office. The building was stone-clad modern build, six stories high. The footprint was large to accommodate the trading floors and operations. Each trading floor was packed with desks and monitors displaying statistics from the global financial markets. Jennifer was an early starter; however, the desks were already full when she got there. She picked up a coffee on the way upstairs. Her meeting with Justin was at 10 AM, which gave her time to clear her inbox and catch up quickly with her team leads. All was well with the systems she managed; all reports were where they were supposed to be, and she was comfortable there would not be any issues to resolve.

Justin was a typical technology lead—highly intelligent with a real passion for computer systems. His desk was full of the latest technology books, and he always had the most up-to-date technology for his phone and devices. His team all looked up to him, and they regularly went out on team events. Each one of them would often be found burning the midnight oil to hit deadlines.

He came into the meeting room with a smile.

"Hi, Justin, is everything up and running this morning?" Jennifer asked.

"Yes, the overnight processes have worked their way through. The support team had to fix a couple of things, but all is good now," Justin replied.

"What was the issue?" Jennifer asked.

"The usual really, the upstream systems sent bad data, which caused our import processes to break, which stopped them until we could get a refeed. It always seems to be the Rates Trading System (RTS) that breaks our whole system. You would think they could send down the right data. Apparently, they made a system change the night before, and it ended up changing the data in the feed file, and it broke our import processes," Justin said.

"How often does this sort of thing happen?" Jennifer asked.

"At least once a week. Sometimes I think they do it deliberately to keep us on our toes," Justin said, looking exasperated.

"I don't think that is the case, I think that being a data and analytics system at the end of the complex chain means that any upstream dependencies have an effect on our system," Jennifer replied. She had seen this type of issue on her other projects and was aware of the realities of trying to pull data together. "What do you tend to do about fixing the issue?" she asked.

"Well, John debugged the import process overnight and figured out the issue and then advised support on what to fix. He deserves a mention at the end of the year. The number of times he is able to fix these issues and get the system running again is worth a promotion," Justin mentioned, proud of his team's dedication and commitment.

"Didn't the import process pick up the issue and enable support to deal with it?" Jennifer enquired.

"No, it showed up in the consolidation process when we pulled the risk together. By that time, it had gone through all the transformations to write the risk out," said Justin.

"No wonder it was hard to work out the issue. Once it had gone that far down the chain, it must have manifested itself in a completely different way to the underlying problem! How did John figure out what went wrong?" Jennifer asked.

"He took an emergency token to log onto production to view the data. He then ran a series of queries across the datasets and narrowed it down. He went through some of the code and found the problem," Justin answered.

"That must have taken some time?" Jennifer questioned.

"It took him about four hours. Two to investigate and then another two to get the source system teams online to send the refeed. All sorted in the end," Justin said, satisfied that his team had pulled the rabbit out of the hat once more.

"What else does John do?" Jennifer asked.

"He is one of our best developers; he is therefore writing the ETL for one of the main processes for Aspen," Justin said.

"After being up all night, I would imagine it is difficult for him to be productive on the project," Jennifer stated.

"He came in late, and we have to manage the third line support on top of development, so we adjust our estimates for work accordingly," Justin said.

"I imagine it pushes them out quite a lot," Jennifer said.

"It does; the big problem that I have is that the users do not see all of this. We go back with estimates for projects, and they do not understand the challenges of doing development, supporting production systems, and coping with the controls around deploying software, etc.," Justin said.

"I think in part you are right. They are under pressure to produce to their own deadlines, and they need an answer to how long development will take. They therefore ignore the how. Having said that, they are in the same situation themselves. They must produce reports, and they have got projects to run. I therefore think that they would be understanding with the right dialogue. Could last night's issue have been diagnosed quicker if the process had been broken down in steps?" Jennifer asked.

"What do you mean?" Justin asked.

"Would there be any way to catch these types of errors in the flow close to where they first occurred?" Jennifer clarified.

Justin thought for a moment. "The flow has to process billions of rows of data overnight, so we have had to spend a lot of time optimising it; if we do not push it through quickly, there are no results to be seen," Justin answered.

"I understand, it is pulling all of the information from the front office systems and calculators. It must be a complex challenge. Having said that, if the data gets through the process to the end and it is wrong, does it not take ages to rerun it as well as ages to find the issue?" Jennifer asked.

"That is true, but quite often errors are only found in one particular branch of the flow. To stop everything because of this would mean that we are delayed every night. With the number of feeds that we absorb, there is more than likely an error in one of them every night," Justin replied.

"So, you push them through for speed and then post process afterwards to fix issues?" Jennifer enquired.

"Yes, mostly," Justin replied.

"OK, so could you add in checks and balances on each of the branches to catch these types of errors earlier and then stop the branch to wait for intervention whilst the rest of the pipeline proceeds?" Jennifer asked.

"The code is all in one big extract transform and load (ETL) processor. It can run in part incrementally, but there are a lot of dependencies between the jobs. The data needs to be built in a certain order to create a clean set, so I am not sure it is as easy as that," Justin answered.

"I know of a way to remove a lot of dependencies downstream in the system and to make it work in a much more incremental way. We used this method of extensibility on a previous project. The overhead on support, the speed of development cycle, and the ability to process data rapidly enabled us to get better results on the service level agreements (SLA)s. This reduced the amount of support outages and gave the teams a much better ratio of development to support. It meant we could spend a lot more time on interesting project work. Would that appeal to you?" Jennifer asked.

"Yes," Justin answered skeptically. "How would you do that?"

"It is called instrumentation; by instrumenting the data pipeline, you are able to pick up on errors before they become a challenge. Secondly, by building an extensible schema, you can add in the information as it arrives. Therefore, if one of the files is late, then the rest have already processed. When the late file arrives, it can be added into the schema to complete the reporting. The key to the solution is embedding data quality alongside the results to provide information to the user about what they are seeing in the results. They also should have the choice to view or use the results based on the information displayed in the data quality dashboard," Jennifer said.

"It makes sense, but we are dealing with huge quantities of data. We have landed it into a big data platform to be able to give us the capacity to process it in time. We can load gigabytes and gigabytes of the data in a few hours and then process it into datasets for reporting. The downstream reports then pick up these datasets. The quantities we are dealing with make it difficult to change things completely. Otherwise, the read processes take ages," Justin said.

"I was talking to Ian Cole yesterday. He mentioned that the country groupings and sectors were feeding through the system from the calculation engine," Jennifer mentioned.

"Yes, they specified that. It has added a lot of size to the information that we already have to process. Not only that, but they seem to change their mind every few days with new mappings. It means we must run through the data into the system again. The team are working long hours to keep up with the requirements. I have implemented a sign-off system now for the change cycle to remove the amount of churn we are getting, otherwise we will never produce any results. The users now write things down and we collate them together; every two weeks we have a planning meeting to discuss the next release in two weeks' time," Justin said.

"Sounds like agile and scrum iterations," Jennifer observed.

"Yes, it is a great way to build discipline in the process," Justin replied.

"Given the timelines, doesn't that cause issues for the users?" Jennifer asked.

"What do you mean?" Justin asked.

"Given the fact that they can only change mappings every two weeks, and then it takes the team three days to process the data through the system. Then they see an iteration of the results every three weeks," Jennifer calculated.

"I told management that these timelines were going to be difficult," Justin said.

"I will ask the same thing to yourself as I did to Ian. Which part of the calculation uses the country groupings and sectors?" Jennifer asked.

"They don't. The BRD specified that they feed through from the calculation engine, so we built it that way," Justin mentioned.

"I said to Ian, would it make sense to add the mappings to the pipeline at the end, so that they do not create a large dependency? That way the iterations can run much quicker," Jennifer asked.

Justin thought about this for a while. "The challenge we have with that is that the lake is slow at running joins with lots of data. We store the information in big tables to take away this challenge. We can then push the information out into the reporting tools to meet the SLA," Justin replied.

"Can you draw up the architecture on the board, as I need to understand it in more detail?" Jennifer asked. She was a little concerned that at this moment Justin was getting a little defensive, and she needed to be able to move his thinking forwards.

Justin went to the board and picked up the black pen. "As you know, we process feeds from all over the organisation into the risk data store. Primarily our feeds for risk come through the risk calculator. This runs a list of calculations defined in the scenario engine and then executes these against the positions coming in from the organisation." Justin drew the risk engine on the board with the scenario manager. "The risk from the risk engine streams into our ingestion engine throughout the calculation process, and we capture it and write it into the lake for consumption. The lake stores it against the run id and writes out Big Tables. The data is written to the lake in logical sequences to enable interrogation by book identifier. On the consumption side, we have created a consumption engine that can send in a list of books, and it returns the rows from the lake. The API writes these out and it plugs into the reporting tools that run ETL to create report sets and reports for the users." Justin produced a diagram as shown on the board (see Figure 3.1).

"I see, so the users only interact with the process to kick off risk runs and then to check the reports at the end?" Jennifer asked.

"Yes, we wanted to give them permissions to read the lake, but they ran huge queries that froze it up, and we had to restrict access. We built them an interface where we can control the resources efficiently to stop this happening and to make sure that the essential processes go through," Justin said.

"I am not surprised. Lakes are designed for massively powerful processes running on large datasets; however, they do not work for ad hoc querying very well, especially for large numbers of concurrent queries," Jennifer replied.

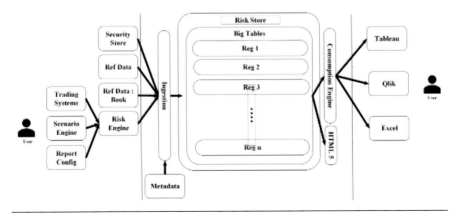

Figure 3.1   The existing Aspen system drawn on the board by Justin.

"They are not as easy as people make out. We were promised huge power at low cost and it is not that easy!" Justin stated.

"I don't think they were designed specifically for flexible ad hoc querying; they work best when you know your indexing, and therefore you can place your data on them appropriately. How do you keep your data from different processes separated?" Jennifer asked.

"We create different areas for the different types of risk that we run," Justin mentioned.

"So, there is no standardisation in the lake?" Jennifer asked.

"No, not really. Each specification we receive is for a different use case. Each one needs different types of reference data on them. It is impossible to standardise," Justin stated.

"You implement each project from scratch without trying to standardise?" Jennifer asked.

"We are able to code the ingestion and the consumption interface really quickly. John did a great job in creating generic modules for this that take an import definition and an output definition and write to the cluster in this way. We sometimes need to write custom ETL to process the data, as it has specific lookups that prevent us from using the generic loader," Justin said.

"If I wanted to combine feeds from two separate business processes into a new piece of analysis, would I need to write code specifically for this purpose?" Jennifer asked.

"Yes, you would, but we rarely do. We have capacity to run the data in a complete form again. With cheap storage that is the flexibility you get," Justin said.

"If the users want a new query, you code something specific for them in the system as part of the change cycle?" Jennifer asked.

"Yes, I have a dedicated team working on these requirements. There is demand beyond what they can manage," Justin said.

"What tools have you got in the reporting and analytics space?" Jennifer asked.

"We have the standard reporting tools, Tableau® and Qlik®. The users own these and pull data out of the interface to feed them. We present the data to them in some custom reporting front end," Justin mentioned.

"Oh, that sounds like a lot of work per report," Jennifer said.

"We have some templates in HTML outputs that meet the specification of the reporting requirements and present the data," Justin said.

"Do the users use it much?" Jennifer asked.

"They use it for official signoff of the numbers. I do not understand why they do not use it more. We are trying to get management to mandate it and take away their access to alternatives, but there is a lot of resistance to it. They know they should be using official systems; they just don't seem to be listening," Justin said.

Jennifer empathised with Justin, she could see where he was coming from and how soul destroying it was to put in all the effort he and his team clearly did to get data to the users, only for it to be seemingly ignored. The gap between the business and IT needed to be filled if this was going to be successful. She needed to enable IT to be more responsive and to meet the real needs of the users, and the users needed to be able to do their job more effectively with the IT systems than they could without it. The issue she could see with Justin and the IT team was that the system was struggling to serve the data that the business needed in the way they needed it.

"Justin, how are the reporting systems coping with the demand on them?" Jennifer asked.

"There is too much data in them generally. The users keep asking for new reports, so we keep extending the schema to enable it to meet the new requirements. The reporting tools are not set up to handle the capacity that is being asked of them," Justin said.

"Have you looked at dividing and conquering?" Jennifer asked.

"I am not sure what you mean," Justin responded.

"In an analytical schema, the more you try to make it be all things to all men, then the worse it performs. The trick is to subdivide the use cases up into multiple schemas to make sure the sets remain pertinent and efficient for the users to use. The outcome should be the minimum amount of reporting sets to meet the needs of the users for functional and non-functional requirements. In my experience, it is rare that a single user needs all the detail functionally and all the grain, so you can break it down into logical sets and build in flexibility," Jennifer said.

"I am still not sure I understand," Ian looked puzzled.

Jennifer took to the white board and grabbed the red pen. She started drawing. "If we can break down the datasets into core data and reporting-specific data, and then we can accept that one reporting schema per project is not scalable, then we can build flexibility into the analytical schemas. It should give us the responsiveness to meet the user requirements." She drew the following onto the white board (see Figure 3.2 on following page).

"Here what I have done is to add user inputs at different stages of the pipeline. Much of these will be automated over time, but the exception management needs to remain as a human-led decision. This prevents the data getting too far down the process before errors are discovered and enables us to iterate and manage upstream and downstream responsibilities more effectively," Jennifer said.

"The second stage is to separate out core models from use-case-specific models to enable us to standardise more effectively. The use-case-specific models need to be kept as add ons to the core data. We then make analytics and report building much more flexible and based around metadata as much as possible to enable them to be built and discarded on the fly. This area of the system will generally

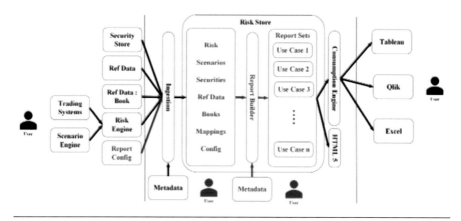

Figure 3.2   Suggested amendments to the Aspen system drawn on the board by Jennifer.

iterate very rapidly during these projects and in the work of the users. We need to enable this to happen to allow the system to flow. Once the process is established, then we can lock it in and manage it in a more structured way. We accept that one reporting schema does not solve all problems, and then we build out as many or as few as needed to fit the business process," Jennifer explained.

"The issue with this is that we end up with many versions of the truth!" Justin replied. "This is against the principles that we are working towards."

Justin had a point—the whole purpose of bringing risk and finance together was so that the data from risk and finance would be starting from the same version of the truth. The reason for doing this was that the regulations were getting tighter around data being consistent, and the regulator was getting much more focused on consistency.

"Justin, do you accept that a tool or system does not exist today to meet all of our organisation's reporting needs in one instance that holds all of the data?" Jennifer asked.

"Yes, the current reporting tools that we use cannot scale to store all of the data in the lake," Justin replied.

"Do you also accept that the data lake can contain all of the data, but it is not responsive enough to meet multiuser querying and workload?" Jennifer asked.

"Yes, that is apparent from what we have experienced and the reason that we built the interface to control the access to the data," Justin replied.

"The only possible conclusion is that we need multiple reporting outputs, or caches, fed from a consistent source. We then need to make sure that the information in the caches is well documented and understood so that when it is used it cannot be misinterpreted. Finally, we need automated tools that test the consistency of the information and present this alongside the output. I cannot think of an alternative to this with current technology and the need to be accurate," Jennifer said.

"When you put it like that, I suppose you are right," Justin accepted. "How do we get from where we are now to have something like this implemented?" Justin was concerned this was more work than he and his team had capacity for.

"Firstly, we need to look at the way the team is currently working. We need to hand over tasks that they are currently doing that are not their responsibility and work with the other stakeholders to pick these up. From my discussions with them, they are expecting to do these anyway, they do them already when you write the reports. You must know they extract all the information and look at it in Excel® and Tableau. This should then take the pressure off the team to start to look at building more extensibility into the overall platform," Jennifer said.

"We will need extensible schemas, processing, querying, and reporting that is controlled and consistent. We will also need to start to embed some of the rules and the mappings into data. We should start with quick wins that help us to move forwards, and then once the momentum builds, tackle some of the trickier jobs," she continued.

"What sort of quick wins are you thinking of?" Justin asked.

"Firstly, we should get the users to maintain report-specific mappings. This will take that load off you and will enable them to iterate much faster. Secondly, we should look to get them verifying the data earlier in the pipeline. They should be able to validate high-level numbers that are coming from the calculators and fix them prior to all of the aggregation and reporting," Jennifer said.

"That will mean restructuring our sprints," Justin said.

"There will be some disruption for the next sprint, which may cost some time. Once the changes are delivered, the project will accelerate, and the time lost will be easily caught back up," Jennifer replied.

"Let me take a look at that, and I will estimate the work required," Justin answered.

"In the first stages, the solution needs to be minimum viable product so that we can get the project moving forwards. We can then look to industrialise and refine it once the project starts to track better and people embrace the new approach," Jennifer said.

"OK, I will look at that and see what can be done," Justin said.

Jennifer felt that they had made good progress for a first meeting, and the changes of approach she had suggested were enough for the technology team to be getting started with. She wrapped up the meeting, and they both left back to their desks.

The next challenge would be to look at the data definitions and data analysis. The information being produced in the specifications would need to be changed, and the way that it was captured would need to be more integrated with the project rather than something external and peripheral.

Jennifer knew that to improve the team's performance she would need to get them to be more focused on the data. From reading the specification processes, it was clear that they were spending time writing mapping documents, but they were not getting the results from these that she would expect. She would need to spend the afternoon looking at the documents produced so that she could identify where the process was breaking down. She had a good idea where this was, but she wanted to find specific examples. From the discussion with Ian Cole, the data was getting introduced into the pipeline at the wrong point. This was obvious, but she would have to spend time with Carl and the documents to understand how they needed to change to improve the process.

Closing Questions

A good DataOps solution will enable you to spend more time on building the system and less on support and heroics. It will be able to flex to meet the needs of the users rather than the users needing to meet the needs of the technology. Here are some questions to think about:

- Are you spending a lot of your time firefighting rather than on value-add activities?
- Did you buy into a technology solution and then fit it to the requirement, or the other way around?
- Is a single tool a large bottleneck in your ability to meet multiple needs?
- Have you had to implement a very rigid contract-based mechanism to bring order to your data and analytics projects between IT and the business?
- Do you have a large legacy of dependencies and side effects that means a large regression is needed for every production release?

Chapter 4

Getting Data Driven

Key Concepts

It is ironic that the purpose of data and analytics is to support the business in making better decisions, yet often the data engineers and technologists do not follow the same approach. One of the key parts of the DataOps methodology is to instrument data to build up enough metadata to help drive design and implementation decisions. Capturing the right metadata is crucial to being able to make decisions on the right technologies to use and to understand where the data fits into the overall solution.

We find that in many projects, profiling is seen as an unnecessary step in the project lifecycle, yet often the data that is captured in this key activity and the knowledge gained is often the difference between the success and failure of a project. It is important that the right data is captured and not just a brain dump of the requirements. This takes an element of understanding of the set-based nature of data in contrast to the function-based paradigm of computer programming. Being able to see requirements and systems in these two frames will enable you to simplify what you are building considerably.

THE FOLLOWING day Jennifer was in early as usual, and the meeting with Carl was set for 9 AM. She had to book one of the external meeting rooms, because all the internal meeting rooms were full. It was always a bit of a treat to be in these. They were set out to impress large corporate clients, and the art and décor were impressive—not to mention the views across the city. There was tea and coffee laid on by default with biscuits. Carl arrived dressed smart casual with his laptop. Jennifer had asked him to take her through the documents that they had produced. They were far too large and complicated to print. They both had their fingers crossed that the audio-visual equipment in the room was compatible with the laptop connections available.

"Carl, can I get you tea or coffee?" Jennifer asked while Carl was busy fiddling with the wires and the AV screen.

"Tea please. I think I have got this working," Carl replied.

On the screen was displayed Carl's desktop. He seemed to have hundreds of spreadsheets represented as icons, with several documents interleaved. He double clicked on the Aspen data mapping document.

"Here is the Aspen data mapping document that you wanted to walk through," Carl said.

Jennifer finished brewing Carl's tea and pouring herself a coffee. She took her seat and viewed the screen.

"Great, I am glad that was easy." Having had many meetings start 15 minutes late due to wrestling with the audio-visual equipment, it was always a relief when it worked first time.

"Thank you for presenting the mapping sheet, I wanted to walk through the process that you are following and to walk through the data that you are capturing in the mapping sheet," Jennifer said.

Carl grabbed his mouse and clicked on the first tab in the spreadsheet. "I will start at the beginning. We receive a business requirements document from Ian's team. In this he identifies the fields that we need for the reports and then the additional changes that are required for the new requirements. He works with the users to define how they should generate these fields. We take the BRD and then start to decompose it into data requirements and add the fields into this column." Carl pointed to a column on the spreadsheet. "This is a list of all the data in the report alongside the expected source, and then containing the transformation that we need to carry out."

"As you can see, there are a lot of fields. For each of the fields we then add the formula to the right, which explains how to calculate it. This is what takes a lot of time to produce. We need to add the information into the sheet and cross-check that all the references have data sources." Carl worked through the other sheets in the spreadsheet, showing that they all connected and had audit trails, etc. "Once this is complete, then we hand this to Justin and the team as a specification," Carl described.

Jennifer could already see some issues with this approach but needed to understand it further before making any suggestions.

"For each of the cells in the report, you have listed out the formula for the cell. During the process, do you look for commonality between the formulas to represent a set of KPIs?" Jennifer asked.

"What do you mean? Each cell represents a different formula," Carl replied.

"Yes, and no—each cell represents different data, but the formula to calculate the cell is the same for each of the cells. Can you bring up the first report?" Jennifer asked.

Carl brought up the first report by clicking on the sheet in the spreadsheet. Everything was nicely laid out in order, and they could see the outline of the report on the screen.

"If you look at the data in the row headers to start with, all of these represent a country. It is not all the countries of the world, but it is a subset of the countries relevant to this report. Each of the countries is grouped by a region, and these regions are then splitting the total result into subsets, which are then ordered," Jennifer described.

"Yes, I can see that!" Carl was thinking that Jennifer was stating the obvious, as he could easily see this.

"Looking across the columns, there is a list of scenarios that represent the model that was used to calculate the number," Jennifer observed.

"Yes, I see that as well," Carl said, wondering where this was going.

"Yet in each of the cells described by the country and the scenario, there is a formula described. The formula seems to be reported for every combination of country and scenario," Jennifer observed.

"Yes, that is so that the programmers know how to calculate each of the cells," Carl explained.

"I understand that you want to make sure that they get the calculations right, but looking at this, and, given that the programmers are removed from the problem, there is a danger that they will code all of these formulas independently. If they do that, they will create a huge amount of complexity. I would like the mapping documents to be as simple as possible with as little duplication as possible," Jennifer said.

"How would we do that?" Carl asked.

"You can do that by breaking down the template into columns of fields. For example, we have country—firstly we need to know what country this is. I believe in this case it is the country of the security or product that was traded. That is one item. The region is another item, the scenario is another item, and all the cells can be represented as the number (risk) that is calculated for a country and scenario combination. That means that the 200 lines in your sheet can be simplified to a list of a dozen or more. This enables the programmer to establish economies of scale. For data projects, the secret is to establish set theory to create simplifications rather than applying algebra for each result, as that creates complexity," Jennifer explained.

"How do we know what we can simplify and what we can't?" Carl asked.

"This is where you need to refer fields back to a conceptual model and to understand the data modelling in more detail. It should be possible to identify the source and the semantics of a field by what it represents. In this case, where it is consistent across the whole of the report, it can be simplified into a term that represents that concept. If it is different across a report, then you need to find the pattern that explains the field so that it can be modelled either as a column or as a formula that generates it," Jennifer explained.

"How would we go about doing that?" Carl asked.

"This is where we need to get the team involved in profiling and instrumenting the data sources," Jennifer explained.

"What is profiling and instrumentation?" Carl asked.

"In your mapping document, you have identified the source to be used for the calculation. We need the team to profile the data in the source to establish the reliability of the data to support the report. If you can establish this, then you can change individual formulas to be a single column, or a column and a lookup. In the process of doing this, you can greatly assist the development teams and the project teams in establishing potential issues that may exist in the data," Jennifer continued.

"That would be a lot more work on top of what we currently do!" Carl mentioned.

"It would be, but the savings in the project lifecycle would be massive. It is much more efficient to find an issue and establish a plan for it in the early parts of a project than it is to find that same issue in testing of the solution. The cost goes up exponentially the further down the project we go. Profiling allows us to enter into projects with a good sense of confidence that we have uncovered unknowns before we start," Jennifer answered.

"We have not done this before in the lifecycle; what would we need to do?" Carl asked.

"Firstly, we need actual test or sample data that we propose to use; we then need to check it for completeness, accuracy, consistency, integrity, precision, and representation. I can show you all of this. It can be done in desktop tools for small data or databases and queries for larger data. Secondly, we need to know about the source—when, where, and how. This can be plotted against the information that we know from the feed. Finally, we need to capture variety—how the data is stored; volume—how much of it there is; velocity—how quickly it is going to be coming at us; and volatility—how often it is likely to change. We need to store this information in the mapping document for the feed. Over time, if we store the information in the right way and instrument the production system, then the knowledge can be used to assist future projects and make the job of implementing new features and solutions easier," Jennifer replied.

Carl was looking a little bit shell shocked. "Isn't it the job of the development team to do this from our mapping documents?" Carl asked.

"The development team are currently the bottleneck in this process, through no fault of their own. The issue is that the quality of the documents that we provide them in the data mapping and business requirements document causes them to have to do all the analysis again. If we can find a better interface between us, then it will take the pressure off them, and they can focus on the complex technical requirements of the project. This will lead to faster development, higher quality, and more feedback from the business, which is crucial for building a collaborative culture," Jennifer said.

"So, do we need to redesign our mapping documents?" Carl asked.

"To some extent. You are capturing lots of the right information to start with. We need to extend what you have to capture some additional information driven from the profiling. We then need to organise it into the right shape to be able to use the knowledge more effectively," Jennifer replied.

"What do you mean by more effectively?" Carl asked.

"At the moment, we do not have a buildup of strategic resources for projects. The information gets captured in mapping documents for a project, and then it gets discarded and done from scratch again for the next project. Meanwhile, within the data governance function, they are busy documenting all the production systems in a secondary set of documentation. If we can join these two processes together, then we can achieve huge benefits for both parties. The documents for lineage, terminology, assets, and fields should be consistent between the groups. It should also drive the data pipelines and be fed back to establish data quality and provenance. This is probably the most fundamental change in the way that we are going to integrate all the teams, and it is driven through instrumentation of processes and the organisation of metadata," Jennifer said.

"It sounds like a long-term project. Given the tight timescales, it would mean big delays to the Aspen project," Carl replied.

"We would not be doing this in one go, that would be huge. We will look to do this in incremental stages of continuous improvement; much like a DevOps team gradually improves its development processes, a DataOps collaboration gradually improves its data processes. This happens over time as teams align their responsibility for maintaining the data that they are responsible for, and it embeds into the organisation's operating model. Over time the data quality and collaboration improve, and it becomes part of the overall process," Jennifer stated.

"What can we do now?" Carl asked.

"We need to start with small steps that over time will lead to large change. There are a few things that we can be working on initially," Jennifer replied. "We need to organise the mapping sheets into a more structured, simplified structure. This may take a little time, because in the process I want to spend some time expanding the skills of the team to be able to support doing this longer term. The sheets need to contain terms that explain fields, a bit like column headings; we can then start to simplify the documents into a smaller list of column headings and formulas, a bit like fitting the data into a pivot table. After that we should be able to simplify the complexity of the mapping sheet to make it easier for the IT teams to follow. This should enable us to get the project moving forwards with increased velocity."

"OK, how long do you think this will take?" Carl asked.

"Looking at the sheet, I think it can be changed in about two weeks to what we need it to be. It should then free up the dependency for the downstream teams that use the documents, and then we can get to embedding longer-term goals," Jennifer replied.

Carl thought that, given the project timelines, two weeks was not too demanding.

"After this there are two main tasks that we need to start. The first is to build a set of structures to hold the metadata going forwards. This will evolve, but it needs to be consistent with the analysis process, linked to the underlying pipeline, and used by the users of the system. The second is to populate these artefacts with the information that is not only going to help us on these projects but is going to help us on future projects and reduce down the amount of work that we have to do for the next change," Jennifer said.

"It sounds quite complicated," Carl said nervously.

"It will be different. Not hugely different, but if we work methodically towards the target and incrementally improve in logical steps, then we can take away the anxiety related to the size of the overall change. The team I worked with when I first joined Saturn have got this working, and on the recent audit for personal data and GDPR, they were able to answer the auditor's questions in a couple of days," Jennifer said.

"Wow, that took our team a couple of months of analysis alongside the IT teams to uncover personal data fields," Carl said.

"Those are the types of benefits and the productivity levels we should be expecting; when we have reached that point, we will be in a good place," Jennifer said.

"Are there any books I can read on this to help me with understanding data in more detail?" Carl asked.

Jennifer thought for a moment; the books that had provided her with most inspiration were Kimball's *The Data Warehouse Toolkit*[1] and *Building a Scaleable Data Warehouse with Data Vault 2.0* by Linstedt and Olschimke.[2] However, it was as important to read these in the context of organising data for consumption as it was to follow them prescriptively. The theory was excellent, and the data modelling patterns were good and useful, but they needed to be abstracted from the books and brought into a data lake architecture paradigm. Despite this, they would provide a good foundation for Carl and his team to start to understand data modelling and design.

"Carl, probably the best two books to improve your knowledge and find a foundation in what you are doing would be *The Datawarehouse Toolkit* by Kimball and Ross, and *Building a Scalable Data Warehouse with DataVault 2.0* by Linstedt and Olschimke. They provide pragmatic experience in understanding data patterns. However, in this project we will not be following them to the letter of the law. The reason for this is that we need to keep a focus on what we are trying to achieve and the technology that we have available to do it with," Jennifer replied.

"What you are saying is that the books provide a foundation of knowledge, but they do not provide the answer? How do we get up to speed on the rest of the knowledge required?" Carl asked.

"It will take some time and experience coming up to speed. We will get there in stages. I have asked Dan Churchill to work with the Aspen team as a mentor and a guide. He has been working in this way for a number of years, and he can assist the team to move forwards, guiding them on the way," Jennifer replied.

"OK, so he will be able to assist us with the mapping documents then?" Carl asked.

"Yes, I will set up a session with Dan, your team, and myself to kick off the initial work of restructuring the templates. Once this has happened, then we can

---

[1] Kimball, R., Ross, M. (2013). *The Data Warehouse Toolkit: The Definitive Guide to Dimensional Modeling,* 3rd Edition. Wiley. ISBN: 9781118530801.

[2] Linstedt, D., Olschimke, M. (2015). *Building a Scaleable Data Warehouse with Data Vault 2.0.* Morgan Kaufmann. ISBN: 9780128026489.

have regular review sessions to see how this is working and to provide guidance and assistance. We have got some examples of the process from my previous projects that will provide you with a good example of this," Jennifer replied.

"OK, so I should wait for you to set up the meeting with the team?" Carl asked.

"Yes, I will do that when I get back to my desk. I want to set some realistic, achievable goals for the group to make changes. I realise this is new to many, but it is important that we find a model that enables the team to work more collaboratively together," Jennifer replied.

Carl acknowledged the need to improve the performance of the team; he was extremely aware of the fact that it was not working well. He did not realise that it would mean some changes to his approach. He felt reassured that it would be for the better but was not sure at this stage what it would entail.

Jennifer and Carl left the meeting and returned to their desks. Jennifer immediately set up a meeting with the data analyst team. This was an important first step for them and the overall project team, and she needed to move fast to organise the mappings into clearer specifications. Once done, this would lead onto the central data governance function. She would need to meet with Karen Lester to start to table the way the team would be working and then start to feed this into the overall CDO responsibilities.

Closing Questions

Being data driven is a key skill of a data engineering team. Here are some questions to think about:

- Do you really know the data that you need to satisfy the requirement?
- Do you know where to get this information from, and is it organised well?
- In your methodology, is there room for data profiling and prototyping?
- Are you able to model the implementation required prior to committing to code?
- Do the technologists on the team use the data-mapping documents that you produce, and do they add value to the development process?

Chapter 5

Controlled Empowerment

Key Concepts

In many organisations we often see large governance programmes not for the purpose of adding value to the business processes, but as vanity projects for CDOs. The resulting effort is often wasted in producing documents sitting on shelves that are out of date the moment they are written. Many millions of pounds have been spent on these efforts, and they should return net benefit. This would help the CDOs to justify their position in the organisation. The organisations that are most successful with data understand this and can implement the cultural change through the business, which gains benefit from the governance being in place. DataOps goals state that governance is an enabler that primarily empowers individuals within an organisation to leverage data efficiently and effectively with the right safeguards in place to help them make the right decisions.

KAREN LESTER, Chief Data Officer (CDO) of Saturn, had been with the banking group for many years, holding senior positions in many operations departments. When the role of CDO came up, she was a good fit for it, due to her diversity of knowledge across the organisation. She could talk authoritatively about the data challenges of each department and was a trusted figurehead for the role.

Her biggest challenge was that the executives within the bank had no real knowledge of data and how to leverage it. They were aware that data was playing an increasing role in the success and failure of organisations, and that to compete, Saturn would have to take a more data-centric approach across all areas. The board's strategy for this was to establish the role of CDO and then have it report into the COO. They assigned a budget that would be spent on setting up the office and hiring key people into it.

Due to regulations, large swathes of that budget were reassigned to departments other than the CDO, with the CDO having oversight. The budget was assigned to document existing processes, and they therefore allocated existing people in those departments into the roles to fulfill the obligations. This was a double-edged sword, as the people filling the roles had excellent knowledge of the systems of the group, but they were not from formal data backgrounds. This meant that the best that could be achieved in reaching the regulatory requirement was a paper exercise, which had worked to varying degrees of success.

A lot of the work completed formed good documentation, but this was not being maintained and was becoming out of date rapidly. The step change that the board had hoped for from data was being achieved inconsistently at best. Awareness of data issues across the organisation was increasing as the focus improved, but the means and the knowledge to fix it was lacking. This added to the pressure on the CDO, who was expected to deliver tangible benefits to the organisation.

Jennifer had met with Karen on her previous projects and had set up the CDO-mandated structures on her projects as part of the overall programme. She had completed the obligations by integrating the governance into the operating model across IT, change, and the business. This meant that the documentation produced by her project teams and business were directly feeding the regulatory requirements. The documentation was linked to the developed tools and therefore was being checked and updated as a standard part of the development lifecycle.

Her aim was to set up the same structure again. This would require her to undo some of the work already carried out on Aspen and the regulatory projects and implement it in a different way. She would need Karen's support to proceed, but also she was keen on helping Karen out in her role. Jennifer was very aware of how difficult it was to meet the needs of the executive committees whilst asking the teams within the organisation to do additional work that they perceived no benefit from.

Her own experience was that if the extra work for governance was correctly organised, the act of doing it would add value to the development process. It brought clarity to the development process and enabled her teams to make factful decisions about architecture, semantics, data flow, and presentation. This only served to improve the communication with stakeholders and the coherence of the solution with respect to the user requirements. It led to better awareness of data quality and reduced the overheads in testing, training, and support. This had led to her team's being able to focus more on developing solutions rather than supporting operations.

She had set up the meeting with Karen's PA for the afternoon of the following day. It was the only mutually convenient spot in their diaries, and, based on her timeline for producing the assessment for Mark Denby and his management team, it was going to be a key input. She had covered most of the other areas that she needed to change with the team, and this meeting with the CDO would assist her in gaining support from management. Jennifer would use the gap between the meetings with Carl and Karen as an opportunity to start writing up the assessment and to catch up with her teams.

$$\bullet \quad \bullet \quad \bullet$$

Karen was based on the operations floor of the bank. She had her own office in the corner away from the lifts. She was seated at her desk when Jennifer arrived.

"Hi, Jennifer, come in and take a seat," Karen said.

The office was set out with Karen's desk and then a small round meeting-room desk in the opposite corner. It had four chairs around it, and Jennifer sat in the corner facing Karen. Karen quickly finished typing and took a seat.

"Hi, Karen, I hope you are well?" Jennifer asked.

"Yes, thank you, and you? Congratulations on your promotion. It was a good call by Mark. I can see this working out well," Karen replied warmly.

"Thank you, Karen; to be honest, I was not expecting it. There were many others on the list in front of me, but Mark said that he was looking for a different approach on his data projects," Jennifer replied.

"I must admit, your existing risk reporting area is one of the most compliant areas within the organisation. Every time we ask for governance information, they seem to provide it without breaking stride. Many other areas take months to produce information, and then the quality and consistency of it is not good," Karen said.

"Thanks; the key for us is that the process of building the system generates the information we send you. It is rare that you ask for something that we do not already have," Jennifer replied.

"The other areas, without naming names, seem to see us as an unnecessary burden on their work. I do not seem to be able to get the right ownership and stewardship of the information that I hoped I could. Most people try to avoid extra responsibilities, and I must admit I even find the subject of debating semantics quite dry! How did you manage to convince your teams?" Karen asked.

"Like I said, we made it part of the methodology. They start using the terms and the subjects within the course of discussing changes, and then they are captured and attached to the process of producing the data. We then have processes in place to make sure this stays in line, because the users are working with the data daily—they feed back issues through the system, and it is all captured together," Jennifer replied.

"That is definitely a model we should look to replicate across the organisation," Karen stated. "There is too much for us to police directly, and it needs the teams to take some ownership. We provided our budget to the teams to put in place the right governance structure, and it all seems to have been used up producing lineage diagrams and downloading database schemas into our dictionary. We have so many terms in there nobody seems to be using it. I was hoping it would provide enlightenment, but it just seems to have added complexity and filled up," Karen was unable to hide her frustration with the lack of progress that many had achieved.

"I think the key to our getting this efficient for the risk reporting was to have a clear structure to the metadata that we wanted to capture. We identified five types of metadata that we needed to manage, and then nine categories of process metadata," Jennifer explained.

"What do you mean by process metadata?" Karen asked.

"This is the metadata that is generated in relation to the implementation of a process—for example, logs, schedules, volumes, sizes, etc. We differentiated this because of the volatility of the information," Jennifer said.

"When you say volatility, what do you mean?" Karen asked.

"One of the big issues with trying to capture metadata in the form of terms, lineage, ownership, models, etc. is that some of the metadata is linked to business process or technical process, and some of it is linked to data. If we cannot differentiate between the metadata related to process and the metadata related to data, then it starts to cause huge amounts of problems. The reason for this is that processes change frequently, not necessarily in their outcome, but in their implementation. People leave, processes get optimised, new processes get requested or implemented; it is in total flux, and for good reason. Having data related to this in the dictionaries means that they become out of date rapidly, or slow the progress of change, or get ignored. The key is to differentiate between these types of data and learn to manage them in the appropriate way. This has been the secret of why my team is able to support the requests you make rapidly with minimum effort," Jennifer said.

Karen was intrigued. "What you are saying is that your team is managing the metadata correctly, and that is the reason that you are able to respond more quickly and more efficiently?"

"Yes, mostly that is correct. The other thing that we have done in the project is to tie much of the data that is needed into the technical processes, so that they become self-describing. When they are changed, the metadata that they are associated with is also changed. This enables us to handle the volatile metadata in a way that is complimentary to its lifecycle. Most of it is useful for communication and for explanation of data.

"What we found before we did this was that the team were spending large amounts of time explaining numbers and data to the users. This was taking them away from improving the process and meant we could not move forwards as fast as we needed to. It was therefore a useful exercise to implement the right governance structure, and the users and the data teams are happier. The users are happier because they are more empowered by the data, and the data team are happier because they can spend more time working on engineering and less time on archeology. So, it is a win-win situation," Jennifer explained.

"Was it hard to set up?" Karen asked.

"It takes time to implement. The right way to do it was to set up the structure and the practice of doing it and then to make sure all future projects follow this structure. The legacy projects can be migrated over time, as and when it makes sense. Data is an infinite game; therefore, you need to set up processes to manage it that stand the test of time. It is not possible to address it with finite thinking. The budget that we received from the CDO initiatives enabled us to set up these processes, and they are serving us well," Jennifer said.

Karen was getting more intrigued by the thinking and whether she could align it to the challenges that she was seeing from other areas. Budget had been spent to produce static documentation to describe an agile process. This was then sitting on the shelf gathering dust whilst the business processes moved forward. By linking the governed data to the change process, then the required governance could be kept in line. This could be the secret to structure the CDO function across the business. "Is the pattern repeatable? I am thinking this could be the key to helping to improve the process throughout the organisation," Karen asked.

"I do not know all of the systems and issues across the bank; however, what we did follows standard logic, so there is no reason why it should not work. The reason I wanted to come and meet with you was to talk through this approach so that I could implement it on the Aspen project, with your blessing. It may mean we have to refactor some of the original documentation that we have completed to this point. However, longer term it should mean that we can improve the information provided," Jennifer explained.

"At the moment, the documentation that we have for these systems is the official information. We would need something equivalent; then we can look to make the relevant changes," Karen stated.

"That makes sense. The documentation you have contains much of the metadata that is volatile. I need to change this to just be the non-volatile metadata and then report the volatile metadata in a different way," Jennifer replied.

"When you say in a different way, what do you mean?" Karen asked.

"The volatile metadata describes processes on KPIs, formats of reports information that is requested by individuals in the business to support marketing campaigns, risk analysis, etc. Over time the focus of these changes—for example, at certain times in the past everyone was focused on buy-to-let mortgages; next they were interested in first-time buyers; then the focus became credit cards and unsecured personal debt. Each time this happens, then the business flexes to provide the new information to the management teams and the regulators. This means they must change data in the systems to support the new analysis. This information can be temporary in nature. Declaring it within the models and the terms adds too much inertia to the process of providing the information, so people find ways around it. This then means the official record becomes out of line," Jennifer explained.

She continued, "In the risk-reporting project, we report this additional information via provenance, or to describe that more accurately, in operations metadata. We keep the core model structured traditionally, because it remains relatively constant. The difference in the amount of maintenance is huge. It took some time to set up the provenance of the system, but once achieved, it reduced the overheads of looking after the metadata to a manageable level. In addition, it empowered the users with additional information alongside their reports. This transparency reduced the amount of support that the IT team had to spend explaining things and improved the conversations we had with the business.

"Historically, the business would find mistakes and then report them back to us. After some time, we were capturing most of the mistakes and telling them. Once this was the scenario, we were able to get them to focus on data quality and the metadata in the system more proactively." Jennifer explained the key reasons for reducing the overhead in managing metadata whilst improving the flow of information and collaboration between the business and IT.

Karen was concerned that by removing the controls around the process metadata, then it would become a free for all. "With the amount of change that you have in the systems, how can you add in the appropriate controls around accuracy, completeness, etc.? We are trying to get to a golden source of data. From what you are describing, this is an agile free for all, where data is changing and being used all over the place," Karen said.

"The challenge is that the demands on the business warrant agility. This means that data is changed and used all over the business to satisfy that demand. The problem with locking down the systems and saying that there is only one way to produce an answer is that it does not change fast enough, and people will find a way to get that answer outside of the controlled systems. If that happens, then you have lost control. The byproduct of this is that the work being done to cleanse information in the systems is lost and stored in spreadsheets and other user-led solutions. The lineage, provenance, and data quality are harder to produce, and it becomes too much of an overhead. By putting in place instrumentation on the iterations of the system, we can capture behaviour and feed it back into the system, improving the quality and reducing future workload," Jennifer said.

Karen was still not comfortable, as this was starting to deviate from the key principle that she had helped to establish that all reporting and information comes from a consistent source. The principle was designed so that the information could be cross-referenced and verified even if it came from different departments. It was also because senior management were frustrated with their meetings being spent where risk and finance figures would contradict each other, and they would waste the time that they should be discussing the way forwards on discussing the validity of the numbers. This was a big driver for CDO.

"The premise of what we are working towards with the lake initiative and the consolidation of the business is a single version of the truth. This seems contradictory to your proposal of a world where people can change information all the time in their own way," Karen said.

Jennifer needed to get the point across that the single version of the core data would be consistent and that the only thing changing would be the way that it was organised for process-led consumption. "They only create sets of data from the single version for their needs; this is for optimisation purposes, but also pragmatically it is the only way to solve the Big Data problem. Recognising that this can create data quality inconsistencies, we add in automated tests for the branches, we provide provenance, and we provide explanations of the data in the reports, as well as showing that data alongside the data-quality dashboard. This empowers people within the official system to get and see what they need.

It takes away their desire to download the information and work on it offline. That means we have greater control of the information within the organisation. This helps with GDPR and other regulations," Jennifer said.

"To paraphrase what you are saying, in order to gain more control, we have to give more freedom?" Karen asked.

"Essentially, controlled freedom in a scenario where we create win-win for all involved, to bring focus and attention to the outcomes that we want to achieve," Jennifer said.

"Do you think that this can be done on the scale of Aspen? Previously within risk reporting, it was a small, tight-knit group. The complexity of the large organisation with competing needs is a difficult prospect," Karen mentioned.

"It is certainly more challenging to get everyone in line and pulling in the same direction. However, it is almost more essential. In my opinion, the only way to work on such a huge quantity of information is to federate and divide up ownership and responsibility, so that everyone is working to provide transparency on the same information. The key is to identify the parts of the information that need to be scoped locally and the ones that have wider organisation reach. For example, certain sets of data are only relevant to finance—for example, tax codes—yet other data like balances of accounts are relevant to many parts of the organisation.

"To support this, we define the scope alongside the data items, which helps us to define where it sits in the organisation. Adding in the type of the data— i.e., process metadata or core data—helps us to differentiate how the individual types of data need to be managed and governed. By doing this, we can organise the data in the governed systems to be useable and defined by the data owners. They will then focus on making sure that the data they own is maintained and documented correctly. I found on the risk-reporting project that as soon as people feel that it is going in the right direction, then they are willing to contribute more, and momentum builds," Jennifer said.

"This model, if it is effective, could well be the answer to the challenges that we have in CDO. If we can prove it out on a larger project than risk reporting and it works, then that should enable us to take it out to a wider audience." Karen was thinking this through. She was facing tough questions around the budget allocated to her programme. Many in the organisation were looking for the programme to show returns, yet all that seemed to happen was that it created more work for people. The work her group was doing was essential to understand information being used and relied upon by the organisation to make decisions; however, there was a need to show tangible returns for the efforts.

She thought it through for a minute. If she could align resources to help Jennifer and to glean the knowledge from the implementation, it would help her team to understand how to roll this out. They could assist and document and provide the shape for other parts of the organisation.

"What help do you need? Can I provide a resource to the project to assist and enable us to absorb the lessons from the implementation?" Karen asked.

Jennifer would be grateful for the assistance, but she was also extremely focused on the tight timelines for the immediate delivery. She needed everyone to focus on this in the early stages.

"How would that work?" Jennifer asked.

"We provide the resource from our team, paid for by us. They would be there to work on the project but also to gain knowledge of the implementation, so that when we want to roll this out wider, we have someone to spearhead that from the CDO," Karen said.

"It would be useful to have additional resources," Jennifer said. "The key in the early stages is to get the project on the trajectory and velocity it needs to be on. That is going to take one-hundred-percent focus on the goals. Once the momentum is in the right direction, then there will time to enable them to contribute wider," Jenifer said.

"That makes sense," Karen said. "How long do you think it will be for you to get to that stage?" Karen asked.

"We have our first milestone in three months. It is the goal to be able to do a dry run of the regulatory requirement. We need to hit that to be able to complete the second dry run before the actual deadline. We need total focus on the first milestone and then the implementation of the changes after that. Once we have assessed where we are at that point, we should be able to then look to provide the input required to the CDO," Jennifer said.

Karen thought for a while. It would make sense to integrate with this, but there were pressures on costs.

"OK, I can commit a resource to help out early on for three to four months, before I need them to write up what they know for the CDO organisation. It would be a great help to the rest of the organisation if this works," Karen said.

"Thank you, it will be a great help. That resource can work with the data analyst team and Carl Hinkley. Dan Churchill is working with this team to provide mentorship and guidance, carried forward from risk reporting. It will be a great help to have an extra pair of hands focused on the deadline and working towards refining the governance processes. It will enable us to build the governance out aligned to the requirements of the CDO as well as meeting the deadline." Jennifer felt genuinely thankful for the offer of help. There was a lot to do, and having additional support could only help.

Karen thought about the current projects and who would be the best fit for this initiative. "James Cramer is aligned most closely to risk and finance and has just finished producing a lineage strategy document. It would be good for him to understand more about the approach that you are following to integrate that into his thoughts," Karen said.

"Thanks, would you be able to introduce us for a conversation? It would be good to meet with him as an introduction," Jennifer requested.

"No problem, I will ping him an email after this and discuss it with him before setting it up," Karen said.

"OK, I don't have anything else that I came to talk about. I wanted to make sure that you were OK with my approach and to change some of the documentation already submitted," Jennifer said.

"Yes, it is OK to change the documentation, and no, there is nothing more from me. I will talk to James after this meeting and let you know," Karen said.

"I will write a summary of the conversation, if you can let me know if the agreed decisions and actions are correct," Jennifer responded.

The meeting wrapped up, and Jennifer felt pleased with the progress she had made. She now needed to get her head down and write up the assessment document that she had promised Mark Denby. She had a couple of days to write it up and get a presentation together before the deadline. She was pleased with her progress towards the goals—not only finding gaps, but moving people forward towards the deadline in the process. The meeting was in the diary for Friday, where she would be presenting her findings and walking through her approach. She wanted to make sure that she could make the points in the right way to gain his support.

Closing Questions

Governance should be an enabler to help people do the right things in a safe environment. If your governance is restricting people and adding to the siloes, then here are some questions to think about:

- Is there a way to make the data maintained as part of the governance requirements a part of the process of building solutions?
- Is the metadata captured in dictionaries really improving the understanding of data in the organisation?
- Is there a way to use metadata to help drive the processes and to leverage it to improve the decisions being made?
- Is there consistency in the information being captured throughout the organisation?
- Does the metadata captured in a previous project get leveraged to make the next project easier?

Chapter 6

Putting It All Together

Key Concepts

Change is difficult. Established patterns of behaviour are often defended against the introduction of new processes and patterns. This is because the new must justify its disruption and really be an improvement on the past. The key objections to a DataOps approach are that many of its parts have been tried in the past and did not work. This is down to two reasons: Firstly, people grasp onto a small aspect of the new and then implement it, not really understanding the full picture, and then claim it does not work. Secondly, the methodology pulls together data tools and techniques that have been around for many years. This can mistakenly mean that people associate them with how they were implemented in the past.

The DataOps methodology is about how these tools and techniques are brought together and implemented that makes the difference. The methodology and approach will take some effort, likely more than you get back in the first project, due to the learning curve and establishing the new tools and techniques. The value starts to build over time and accumulate, making the second, third, and fourth projects much easier than if you had not implemented the solution. In one project that we implemented for a key client, the metadata that we captured for it meant that a subsequent project could be completed in a third of the time.

J ENNIFER SPENT a lot of time condensing her notes from the meetings. Each observation would need to be collated into higher-level topics to present to Mark and the management team. She would need to be able to present them in a balanced way to win support. She was expecting some resistance from the established managers, who approached their projects in a different way. She needed to cost each change and then present the benefits of implementing it as well as the risks. Her time was spent writing up the details and presenting a detailed document and a management summary. There would only be time to work through the management summary in the meeting, but the background needed to exist for her to have credibility if she were challenged.

She would present the findings to Mark on the Friday and then to the management team on the Tuesday. Mark was keen to review the findings first to be able to offer his support to the changes. Jennifer sent through the presentation and the document to Mark on the Thursday evening in time to meet with him on the Friday. Not unusually, despite the late hour, he acknowledged the message with a "looking forward to catching up" reply.

The meeting was early Friday, so there was little time to review the information before the presentation. Jennifer got in early to prepare and to rehearse the information in the presentation and to clear any outstanding issues from the night before. The 8:30 start time soon approached, and she headed across to Mark's office. Tina sat waiting. "Hi, Jennifer, how are you? Can I get you a coffee?" she asked.

"Yes please, could I also have a glass of water?" Jennifer replied.

"He is expecting you," Tina replied.

Jennifer took her cue to go in.

"Hi, Jennifer, thanks for sending through the report last night. I worked through it and it all reads very well," Mark said.

"Thank you, Mark, I wanted to stay true to what worked on the risk reporting project and to enhance it where there are different challenges," Jennifer replied.

"You have captured a lot of good points here, and you seem to have a lot of people on side. Karen spoke to me after your meeting, and she is very enthusiastic about your plans. There are a couple of presentation points that I would like to suggest. It will help you to win approval from the other managers on the team. I will spend some time going through each member of the team and the likely areas of resistance," Mark said. He knew that he needed to get this approach approved as much as Jennifer did, as the pressure was building. Senior management were under pressure themselves, and they needed to get the organisation to move forwards more effectively.

Mark started to go through each of the management team members who would be attending the meeting on Tuesday. "Firstly, Gary Jefferies; as you know, he manages the staff and the operations of the group. His primary concern is going to be on procedure and approach to support his budgeting process. You will need to get approval for the CDO resource to make sure that it does not throw off his costs and forecasts," he explained.

"Next, there is Brendon Straight, who heads up equities technology. Like his name, he tends to tell you what he thinks, which some people take as a slight, but he genuinely is a good sounding board. He used to manage the reporting for the equities business area before I consolidated it under your role. He therefore will have a say on any changes that you make. I listen to him, as there is normally a genuine risk or issue in what he says," Mark continued.

"Chris Way looks after rates technology; he has been within that group for a long time, rising up through the ranks. He has a good relationship with the business built from his consistent delivery and support. He is well respected. He, like Brendon, is keen to see his reporting done well and believes that he should own it. Yet it is the area where the rates group has struggled to be able to deliver. He has embraced new technology but has struggled with it and has had a number of the vendors in an awkward position over the lack of performance of their systems," Mark explained.

"Was it the vendors who had issues?" Jennifer asked.

"Hard to say; the products on paper claim to be scalable and have huge performance, but there is always an extra dimension to the benchmarks that the vendors produce. It is hard to choose products based on the marketing, and it is hard to completely prove them out before using them," Mark said.

"Next, Jason Foley runs our FX group. He has been with Saturn for two years. He came in from a major rival. In his first year he has moved the platform on to incorporate new ideas. He was recommended by the business, who knew him before. He is loyal to what he knows and is well respected," Mark continued.

"Stephen Chester is heading up credit. He, like others, has come up through the ranks. He probably has the biggest challenge with data of all the above in terms of the diversity of it and the quantity, although lots of it is slower moving than the other business areas. It is harder for him to deal with data quality, and he has set up a lot of stats and information to improve things," Mark continued.

"Within functions IT, there is Kirsty Wright and Peter Low, looking after finance and risk systems, respectively. Both are dealing with a lot of challenges with data. They both receive lots of data from around the organisation and need to consolidate it to be able to produce accounts and group risk numbers. They, as you know, have deadlines to produce the answers each day, or each month / quarter / year. The data that they produce goes out into the public domain and therefore comes under increased scrutiny. You probably know the risk area well, based on your previous role. Finance has challenges on making the numbers add up, as it involves real money, and they need to be precise and fix all upstream issues," Mark continued.

"Thank you. What do you think are going to be the main objections to the recommendations I have put forward?" Jennifer asked.

"You are always going to get opinions," Mark said. "The most vocal in the group will be Brendon Straight and Chris Way. Brendon is genuinely someone who likes to understand things, so he will question for that purpose. Chris will probably be a little more targeted. Jason will provide input based on his experience and dismiss some things as not his concern. What you recommend makes a lot of sense to me, so I would put it out there and take in the feedback. We can circle back after the meeting to consolidate the views," Mark said.

Jennifer felt reassured that she could present the information with confidence of Mark's support. She knew most of the other managers but had only had direct dealings with a few of them. Tuesday's presentation would be stepping into the unknown for her, as she knew her approach was breaking from the norm.

Mark and Jennifer spent the rest of the hour fine-tuning the wording and the presentation of the points to smooth off some of the sharper edges and to focus some of the points. The theme, the actions, and the approach remained the same, which came as a relief to Jennifer. She believed in what she had worked effectively in the past. She took down a list of edits and changes back to prepare the presentation for the management meeting.

•   •   •

Tuesday could not come around soon enough for Jennifer. She needed to present the changes and to work through the objections to enable her to move forward at speed. She had a deadline to hit. She felt nervous, which highlighted the fact that she did not know the management team well at this stage, and she was unsure of the reaction to her proposals.

On the way to the meeting, she bumped into Chris Way in the corridor. "Hi, Chris," Jennifer said. "Hi, Jennifer, I see you have the poison chalice. How are things going?" Chris asked.

Jennifer sensed the underlying theme which gave away Chris's thoughts on the reporting and analytics. "Very well, thank you, a lot to do, but at this point achievable, with some focus. How are things with you?" Jennifer asked in reply, trying to move onto something else.

"Very good; the team have worked harder than any other team this year. We have just rolled out version three of the trading system. Lots of new features for the business to use. Took a lot to get it over the line," Chris replied. "Using real-time technology and instant messaging, we are going to give our traders competitive advantage. Much more complicated than the big data stuff, where half of it does not work, and the rest is point and click."

Jennifer realised that the sooner they could get to the meeting room the better, so she increased her pace and started walking with purpose. The rest of the walk to the meeting room was completed in silence, as she steeled herself for the presentation.

When she arrived, Gary Jefferies was setting up the conference line. Mark had mentioned that the heads of IT in Asia and America would be dialing in.

Jennifer poured herself a water and went about connecting her laptop to the conference screen. The system, although temperamental, seemed to welcome her this time. Her screen showed and the presentation appeared. The other managers started filing into the room and taking their seats. Mark was last to join and took his seat at the end of the conference table, with Brendon and Gary on either side. Asia and America had filled the rooms on time, and it was all set up.

Mark opened the meeting. "Welcome everyone. Thank you for joining. As described in the agenda, Jennifer, who will introduce herself shortly, is consolidating the data aggregation and reporting for the organisation. It is a big job, given the importance of data and analytics to this organisation to enable us to manage risk, understand our customers, and optimise the organisation to increase revenues and profitability. I asked her to complete an initial assessment of the landscape in her first couple of weeks," Mark said

Jennifer was thinking it was her plan that Mark had gone with, but she understood why he was taking responsibility for it.

Mark continued, "The purpose of this meeting is to walk through the findings and to provide constructive feedback on the plans. Without further delay, I hand you over to Jennifer to present her findings."

"Hi everyone, thank you for your time to walk through the findings. I hope that you find what I present logical and sensible, given the increasing focus on the reporting and analytics area, and I welcome your feedback," Jennifer explained. She then quickly introduced her background and her previous projects.

After the introduction, she reached the core of the presentation.

"I have split the presentation into the following sections:

- Requirements flow
- Data-driven analysis
- Data-driven design
- Extensible platforms

- Collaboration
- Embedded governance and structure."

She paused briefly to take a sip of water and to take in the room. All was quiet and attentive; the topics themselves did not mean a lot, the key was the implementation.

"One of the big challenges that we have on the Aspen project is the quality of the requirements coming through the standard methodology. The problem that we have is that they only capture the part of the system that produces the reporting. They do not capture the part where the users need to interact with the system. We therefore are building a system to report information and not a system where the users use the information that we report. There is a subtle, but important, difference here, but the net effect is that the users end up downloading the data from the reporting system and then working with it offline," Jennifer described the first point. "I am therefore making changes to the process to align it to the clear SCOPE process that we have used effectively on risk reporting. This will expand the requirements into capturing the interactions with the user. This is the data they need to leverage to be able to use the reports. The SCOPE process breaks down as Storyboards, Content, Output, Process, and Estimate. It captures additional information key to data projects that the existing business requirements process does not capture," Jennifer said.

Chris took this as his cue to ask a question. "So, what you are proposing is to download the data into the users' hands so they can play with it in Excel®?" He laid his trap, waiting for it to be sprung.

"No, that is not what I said, I said the requirements process does not capture the reason why they currently download the data from systems into spreadsheets and then develop their own eco system away from IT. With a controlled process in place to capture these requirements, then we should remove the need for them to continue to do this," Jennifer replied.

"We tried that previously and they just went off and did their own thing," Chris replied. "In the process they kept breaking the batch by running their downloads at the wrong time," Chris replied.

"That is why the SCOPE process will capture the requirement and satisfy it as part of the project, so it can be incorporated on our terms rather than them feeling that they have to set it up themselves," Jennifer replied.

Brendon decided to step in, "So what you are saying, Jennifer, is that if we capture these requirements and satisfy them, then we will remove the need for them to download the data into Excel. Does that not add a lot more work onto the project?" Brendon asked.

"Yes, and no," Jennifer answered. "Firstly, the work will be done anyway. The requirement exists for a purpose. That purpose is that the users need to trust the data. They are going to put their energy into making sure it is right. That energy can either be directed into the project or away from the project. I personally would prefer that their energy be focused in towards Aspen than I would to have it focused on building compensating controls. The SMEs of the data are the business users—they are the only ones who can help us get this right. The morale and productivity of the IT team is dependent on their input, and through collaboration like this, then the outcome is achieved," Jennifer carried on.

Brendon continued, "That still does not explain how the additional work can be achieved."

"Firstly, we capture the requirement, we then add it to the list of items to be prioritised for the project and then work through in collaboration with the users to work out which of the new requirements are most important, which can be satisfied, and how. It may be that short-term fillers are implemented and signed off, and a longer-term item would be added to the backlog to refactor the solution when the time is right," Jennifer continued.

"What if they do not prioritise the refactor. They never do on my projects. We have to exaggerate estimates to be able to buy time for our guys to implement important upgrades," Stephen contributed to the conversation.

"That is due to the lack of trust. Agile is built on trust, and therefore you need to build it over time. The goal in the early stages of the project is to build the trust through delivery of what people need. As trust grows, it is easier to have the conversation about the needs to refactor," Jennifer replied.

"We did agile on our project, and the user base kept changing their minds. The issue was that each change of mind required different data to what they had before, which took months to source and refactor the models and the tools. It meant we had to go back to a more formal requirements process," Stephen continued.

"That is because data is like that. Once a user sees what they can get, then they want the next set of results to follow through their analysis—it is only natural. That is why drill downs and drill throughs are so popular. The purpose of the clear SCOPE process is to identify their needs and therefore make sure that you can anticipate the next requirement in the list. That way you can build a solution that can respond and react to the users' needs, therefore maintaining their engagement," Jennifer replied.

"How do you get the data tools to respond that quickly?" Stephen continued.

"I will come to that later in the presentation," Jennifer responded.

"OK," Stephen replied.

Jennifer paused for a moment waiting for the next question; when none came, she moved on.

"Once we have collected the requirements through the SCOPE process, we will use data analysis to instrument, profile, and verify that the SCOPE is achievable. This is achieved through capturing the size, shape, and quality of the data, as well as verifying that it is timely. We will add profiling to the data analysts' jobs so that they can find data errors early and highlight data quality challenges to make sure that we are handling the complex risks at the beginning of the project," Jennifer explained.

"Jennifer, that sounds like a lot of analysis to do up front. Can you manage the delay in the project?" Peter asked.

"Peter, can we afford not to do it? We need to know if the data will support us to achieve the shared outcome. If it does not, then we need to know. In most cases there are always workarounds; however, those workarounds tend to involve authoring new data or using other data sources to support the requirement. That is not a decision that the IT team is authorised to make. We therefore need to present the analysis back to the steering group to make the call. Without the analysis it is impossible to present the challenges objectively," Jennifer said.

"Isn't up-front analysis and agile a contradiction?" Chris stepped in.

"Not in this case. Data is not like building applications. Application features are generally additive with little cross-over. New pages and features can be bolted on to existing frameworks. Data does not work that way. If you bolt data onto existing data, you tend to create duplication. That then leads to inconsistency and poor-quality outcomes. You need to understand the characteristics of the data before you try to join it all together. It helps you establish if the data will support the conceptual design before you implement the requirements in expensive systems," Jennifer explained.

"So, you are saying that the project will run as a waterfall project?" Chris continued.

"No, that is not what I am saying. I am saying that several sprints will be dedicated to what I call data prototyping, asking the question, will this data support the requirement drawn out in the SCOPE? We will use rapid data tools to prototype and provide roughly the same features that the production system requires to check that they will work. Once the data has been established to meet these requirements, then it can be confidently industrialised into a production solution. Where DevOps has demonstration sprints, DataOps has the same using data to show the possible and to learn early what will work and what will not," Jennifer continued.

"What happens if it does not fit?" Peter asked.

"Firstly, it is useful information to have before you reach the critical implementation. Secondly, there are a lot of workarounds available for data that can be put in place. For example, building a mapping table, building additional reference sources, creating data maintenance processes that will support feeds. All normally require the business to own the data solution. Hence it is a good conversation to have at the start of the project. The information gathered from the process I am describing will contribute to the project team's data awareness, which will lead us to a place where we can share a common understanding of the constraints and enable us to work towards consistent vision of the landscape and the required solution. This is the only way, in my opinion, to run these projects and to build collaboration," Jennifer continued.

"What happens when they shoot the messenger?" Chris added. "Users don't like someone who stands in their way."

"I have not had that experience; generally, the users I have dealt with in the past have always wanted there to be a solution more than they wanted to create an issue of problems," Jennifer replied.

"The front office world is a little less compromising than the reporting world," Chris continued.

"That has not been my experience with front-office," Jennifer repeated. "Before coming to Saturn, I was responsible for front-office technology for a trading business. All users want to feel empowered with information to make decisions. Data analysis provides that level of clarity and empowerment," Jennifer continued. This seemed to quieten Chris down, and he left the floor clear.

Jennifer looked around the room to see if anyone else was due to ask questions, but there was no one, so she moved onto the next point.

"The information gained will be collated in an organised way inside a meta-data hub fed from the templates that we will set up. It can then be used to support design decisions. If we understand the flow front to back, we can model it. We can then test the models against the user requirements and the underlying solution architecture. The ability to do this enables us to have an informed discussion about what can and cannot be achieved, what is easy and what is hard. It enables us to work with the users to determine the priority of their use cases," Jennifer added.

"In my experience," Brendon raised, "most of the challenges come from the technology stack. It does not live up to the complications of the banking industry, and therefore does not support the amount of flexibility that we have within our data flows. When we raise this with the users, they do not understand and just escalate if we say that we cannot do things."

"That is why it is crucial to work with the data. I find that the more I work with facts and information, the less that emotions can get in the way. With facts, everyone can work through the problem and focus on the solution," Jennifer answered. "In a previous project that I worked on, the analysis that we did highlighted that the requirement the users had provided would require us to procure two petabytes of data storage. When we played this back to the steering group, they quickly deprioritised the request and focused on something that could be achieved."

"If I run my projects with this amount of analysis, we will never get anything done!" Chris added.

"If you do not, then how much budget is wasted on implementing solutions that on paper will never work!" Jennifer retorted, getting a little more aggravated by Chris's constant efforts to undermine her.

"A lot of the data systems work perfectly OK one minute, and then the next they just stop performing!" Chris added.

"That is the point of collating the information. It is better to be informed about the time when the systems will fail to scale and be able to proactively manage them, rather than treating everything as a crisis," Jennifer responded.

"Jennifer, do you want to explain how we can do that based on the methodology?" Mark asked.

"Sure. From my experience, data requirements change significantly over time. What someone wants this week will be different to what they want next week. The only way to respond to it is to build flexibility into the design. The data flow information that we capture will enable us to separate concerns into data and processing. Organising the data flow effectively enables us to stay agile and flexible. Over the next year we will need to move data and processes around to be able to build more flexibility into the platform. This can be achieved to a certain extent in the short term through using placeholders, which will be short-term tools that exhibit the right patterns into the design. If we implement the right patterns, then we can incorporate change and flexibility into the solution.

"To add to this, we will look to make the platform data driven, so ideally in most cases we can empower the users to make the changes necessary. To make sure that this remains inside the control and governance structures, then we will differentiate logical groups of data—i.e., core data that does not change as requirements change, reference data which is used for fleshing out the core data to provide insights, and what I call process data that is used for structuring specific requirements. By understanding this, we can support most changes that the users ask for flexibly and efficiently in the platform," Jennifer added.

"So, we have done the requirements and the analysis and then the design, this does not sound agile to me," Chris added.

"You have all heard of DevOps?" Jennifer asked.

"Yes," everyone responded.

"Well in DevOps, you lay foundations of continuous integration, continuous build of software," Jennifer explained. "In DataOps you need to lay different foundations with the steps I am describing here. Once established, then lots of the steps do not need to be done again. They get added to, over time, but the velocity of the team speeds up as the foundations start to build," Jennifer added.

"We used DevOps in the reporting project for rates and it just got bogged down," Chris added.

"The foundations of DataOps and DevOps are different. This is because DataOps is dealing with mutable resources—i.e., data, it changes. DevOps tends to work because applications are immutable in the main. The secret to DataOps and agility is to focus on eliminating dependencies. That is achieved by organising data effectively," Jennifer replied.

Jennifer sensed that the heat of resistance was starting to wane. The energy and arrogance of Chris was starting to lose its power within the room. People were starting to look more engaged and keener to hear more. Mark's body language, although she considered him a great poker player, was looking more relaxed.

There were two more items to deliver to provide a full walk-through of the proposed changes that Jennifer was looking to make.

"The next item is to get data and analytics in front of people early and often to help build collaboration. The issue with data and an environment where trust is running low is that people do not know what they want, what they need, or what is possible. Any one of these mean that once you do deliver, they will realise that what they asked for is different to what they should have asked for. Capturing this early means that there is enough time in the project lifecycle for you to respond and provide what they need.

"The second reason for doing this is that by exposing data to the users and putting together the reports they require, you can share challenges within the data. Often it surfaces poor data quality and missing links, fields, or synchronisation issues. Being able to share these issues helps to build collaboration in the solution and shares the ownership of data problems. It helps the users to understand the challenges in the data and helps them to have realistic expectations of what needs to be done to provide a solution," Jennifer explained.

"What happens if the users then think that the demonstrations and sharing of data is something that they can have immediately after you present it?" Jason asked.

"There are two mitigations for this. Firstly, once DataOps is up and running, then there will be processes to rapidly migrate tactical solutions into production solutions. This will take weeks and not months. Before it is, the mitigation is good communication—being clear with the users what is possible and what is not given what you show them. It takes some courage to have the difficult conversations up front. I have always found users are keen to share their challenges, and they want you to move to a point where they feel that you understand them. By using prototyping with them, then this starts to become possible," Jennifer explained and looked around at the engaged audience. No questions were forthcoming, so she moved onto the final point.

"The final focus for the team is to make the process self-describing and to integrate the governance and control into the process and not outside. This takes time to achieve, but data quality and governance is an infinite game and not a finite game. Data is continually updated and added to the solution, and therefore the opportunity for issues is ongoing. If we code and build the platform defensively, then we will be able to manage quality as part of it rather than as an afterthought and a set of late nights for our support teams." Jennifer could not resist a small jibe at the macho culture that she had endured during the last couple of hours. The culture of heroes' always blaming outside forces and highlighting themselves as knights in shining armor, working all night for the good of the cause, frustrated her when a solution was possible to remove the issues in the first place.

The management team spent the rest of the meeting discussing the points in a little more detail, going through the nuances and the implications. As the discussion curtailed, Mark stepped in to close the meeting.

"I would like to thank Jennifer for presenting her approach to the Aspen project. We should all look to be assisting her in the success of her plans and to learn from the approach, to see what works and can be applied to our own teams. It is important for all of us that this is successful, as data and analytics has an ever-increasing focus from the executive teams and down through the organisation," Mark concluded.

Everyone took it as a cue to leave the meeting and start to move on towards their schedules for the rest of the day. Jennifer collated her materials and disconnected her laptop from the display. Mark stayed behind as everyone left.

"Jennifer, thank you for that. I appreciate that it was quite a difficult audience. People are always a little insecure when they are presented with changes from what they have known. What you propose here is important to our future. I felt it important for you to be able to present to the rest of the audience and become a peer to the other managers," Mark mentioned.

Jennifer did feel like she had gone 10 rounds with a heavyweight boxer. On the other hand, she felt happy that she had come out the other side of it on top and with a clear mandate to move forwards. It was an important step forwards for her and her team.

"Thanks Mark, I appreciate the support. It was a tough audience, but I think we moved it forwards, and their acceptance allows me to progress the plans with confidence," Jennifer responded.

They left the meeting room together and headed back to the IT floor to continue the rest of the day. Jennifer would be consolidating the feedback and sending out her presentation to the team. The focus now was on the implementation and the looming deadline that they needed to make.

Closing Questions

Have you thought through your DataOps journey? Here are some questions to ask yourself:

- What are going to be the key challenges that you will face in adapting your methodology?
- Is there a way to introduce the change in a small way and grow it out from there?
- Are you prepared for the old coming back and fighting you? Culture eats strategy for breakfast.
- Have you got a strategy for winning over the hearts and minds of key people?
- Are you able to break down your projects to deliver value early and build to help people see the value of the change journey?

Part II

Delivery

Chapter 7

A Focus on Plans

Key Concepts

By understanding the data pipeline and organising the data and processes correctly, it is possible to iterate a data project. In many organisations, we see that they struggle with this, and their flagship data warehouse projects start to get into three-monthly release cycles, where much of the effort is tied up in regression testing and handling side effects. This does not meet the requirements of dynamic organisations to make decisions rapidly and effectively. Typically, executives want management information in hours or days; waiting three months can be the difference between being successful or not. It is critical then that the delivery of pipelines is broken down effectively, and processes that need to iterate fast are put close to the change agent. It is also important to break dependencies where they do not need to exist. The key to doing this is to put in place the right building blocks that perform the right functions, even if they are not strategic building blocks in the first iteration.

Jennifer walked back to her office, relieved that she had made progress. At times during the meeting, she had had to rely on her inner strength to get through. She was confident in her knowledge and experience, having successfully delivered many projects in the past; however, she had not been put on the spot quite so persistently in the past. There were some good points raised, and she needed to incorporate them into the presentation before sending it out.

The rest of the day would be spent catching up with the team to get a feel for where they were in relation to the timeline. They would have had time to start implementing the plans, and it was important to capture the feel for where they were and how they were feeling about the deadline. Most important to Jennifer, she wanted data from Carl's team about the data flows and the quality of the data and to hear from Ian's team on the enhanced specifications and Storyboards. Jennifer called Ian and arranged to meet in the coffee shop on the ground floor.

She ordered a latte and Ian had tea. "How have you been getting on with the Storyboard process?" Jennifer asked as they sat down at a table away from the crowds.

"Quite well so far; we have got the main processes that the users follow documented quite well. We are just waiting on the compliance users to agree their processes before we can finalise the documents," Ian said.

"That sounds good; what are the main differences that you have found?" Jennifer asked.

"I didn't realise how much checking, adjusting, and verifying of the numbers actually goes on," Ian mentioned.

"What sort of things?" Jennifer enquired.

"There are a lot of numbers that come down from the legacy systems that do not have the right categories to support the format of the report requested. They must manually map some of the data into the correct categories. The business rules for this regulation seem to be different to the rules of how the business works," Ian said.

"Go on," Jennifer encouraged.

"To support the reporting, they need to drill into the detailed information and either write logic or apply some business rules," Ian continued.

"How are they currently doing this?" Jennifer asked.

"Historically, they would ask for downloads of the data and would do it manually with lots of checks and balances. They have a complete set of procedures that they follow and a set of plans that they implement based on this," Ian replied.

"Is this captured in the Storyboards, and did you include the data required to support this in the dictionary?" Jennifer asked.

"Yes, it has been drawn up and added into the template you provided," Ian responded. "It is amazing how much work that they need to do to verify and make the submissions accurate."

"Does it make sense how a reporting dataset would never support the requirements?" Jennifer asked.

"Yes, it means the work that we did to support the reports was missing a lot of detail. The problem that I see is that to implement all of the logic and processes that they do is too much for us to complete and still hit the deadline," Ian continued.

"Probably," Jennifer replied, "but having this knowledge will enable us to plan the interfaces to the users better, to negotiate how we support them, and to make sure that we can incorporate the data and business rules in future iterations."

"How will we negotiate the position?" Ian asked.

"We will work with them to define the right interfaces and the right processes, factoring in what we can do in the time available and what they can do in the time available," Jennifer said. "Previously, there was no discussion and no understanding; therefore, they chose to ignore the system and go it alone. By providing them with better support, we can build better relations and work together, each using our strengths to solve the problem," Jennifer explained.

"I can see how that could work. It would help our relationship if our solution helped them. Previously, I think they only told us what they wanted because they needed to produce results from our official system to please the audit and the regulator," Ian mentioned.

"In part you are correct. The secret to our success lies in collaboration. This does not normally occur in formal top-down processes—it lies in working towards common goals and seeing benefit in working together," Jennifer continued. "Have you got the information that you have collected so far, so that I can review it?" she asked.

"Yes, I will send it to you after the meeting," Ian replied.

"When do you expect to get hold of the compliance information?" Jennifer asked.

"They should send through the information by the end of the day," Ian replied.

"OK, thanks; can you send that through once it arrives?" Jennifer responded. "And have you provided the additional requirements for data down to Carl to read?" Jennifer asked.

"Yes, he has been kept informed as and when we have confirmed the information," Ian replied.

"Great, I am due to meet him next to see where he has got to," Jennifer replied.

They sat and chatted for 10 more minutes before heading back upstairs. Jennifer enjoyed finding more about her new team, and the last couple of weeks had been quite intense for the usual informal opportunities.

Jennifer was keen to review the data that Ian and his team were due to present. The sooner she could get her arms around the full scope the better. It was clear, as she suspected, that there was a lot more to delivering Aspen than the BRD was providing. Having the full size of the challenge was key to prioritising the teams' work and planning the iterations. She had half an hour to spare before her meeting with Carl, so she started extending the backlog with the information she had gained from Ian.

She was meeting Carl in the coffee shop again. They were getting to the end of the day, and it was close to closing time, so it was nice and quiet. She grabbed a water and got Carl a tea.

"How has it been going?" she asked as they took their seats. The coffee shop had just been renovated, and they had invested in some more comfortable sofas. It provided a great place to have a more relaxed chat.

"It has been going well. Dan has been helpful in guiding us on what to look for. The team has been working through identifying the proposed sources of data, identifying where they are available, and reviewing them. Some, as we knew, were reliable sources of information; others are really poor quality and are not going to support what we need to do. There is also a timing issue with one of the reference data systems. Security Store does not master the data and send it out at this stage in its evolution. It collates data, mostly overnight from all the feeding systems to create a master record. The problem that we are going to have is that the risk process will be sending us the data with the securities that have been created that day, yet our feed from Security Store will not include them," Carl mentioned.

"That's worth knowing," Jennifer said. "Have you managed to find an alternative?"

"The data is entered in the trading systems, so everything we need can be sent down with the risk. We are talking to them to get this arranged. All have existing outputs except the rates system; we have asked for a meeting, but we are struggling to get a dialog with them," Carl described.

"How do we plan to send the information down?" Jennifer asked.

"Based on advice from Dan, we asked for the securities and the relevant data to be sent alongside the feed of risk with common identifiers so we can join it up later," Carl responded.

"OK, that is good news," Jennifer responded. "How do we merge the information with Security Store?"

"That is the tricky thing. They do not have common ids, and Security Store does not send down the trading system id. In most cases the CUSIP and the

ISIN are included in the feed, so we can look to join them once the new data comes through from Security Store. However, there are two issues. We have found cases where the front office CUSIP or ISIN is not keyed in correctly and other cases where there is no CUSIP or ISIN provided," Carl said.

"How often does this happen?" Jennifer asked.

"Fairly infrequently, but enough to mean that we need to find a solution," Carl said. "In one case, there was a big, structured trade with no CUSIP or ISIN. The risk was quite large and was offset by lots of vanilla hedges that had been populated. If we missed it, then the risk of the book would have been seriously misstated," Carl said.

"OK, it is good to know. There is a pattern that we can use to fix this based around master data management and a data quality firewall," Jennifer said.

"Master data management. Isn't that a huge thing that Security Store should handle?" Carl asked, starting to get concerned.

"Well yes, ideally; however, as you have pointed out, it is not providing what we need when we need it. That is the challenge of master data systems that are in the early maturity. They are acting as reference MDMs rather than masters. When they act as masters, then we will be OK; however, as with all reporting systems, we need to implement scaled-down patterns in the interim to fix up the data until we can get a synchronised feed. I will add this to the backlog," Jennifer said. "Anything else that you have found?"

"After running profiling on the data to support the reports, it looks like most of the classifications in the reports are different to the ones we use internally. The rules for generating and classifying by industry sector and country are subtly different. This means that we are going to have to build our own classification," Carl said.

"What is the scope of this?" Jennifer asked.

"What do you mean?" Carl replied.

"Well, does this classification only exist for these regulatory reports, or is it consistent with all regulatory reports?" Jennifer asked.

"Why is that relevant?" Carl asked.

"It will determine how we choose to implement the solution. If it is consistent with all reporting, then we should look to centralise the classifications; if it is purely for these specific reports, then we should look to build them into the reporting metadata," Jennifer responded.

"What is reporting metadata?" Carl asked.

"Reporting metadata is the data used to collate, order, group, and format reports for display. It should be applied as close to the users as possible, as it tends to be the thing that drives how they want the output. However, it is important not to put it in the reporting tool as default. If we do this, then it needs to be duplicated for every one of the reporting instances, and if it does become standard across many reports, it will take a while to extract it and put it in a central repository. If we can extrapolate the logic, then it will make it much easier to use it, make sure it is consistent, and run quality checks against it," Jennifer responded.

"I think the problem that we have is that the users are working on the mapping and extrapolating the right classifications. Therefore, it is hard for us to build the specification for the rules," Carl mentioned.

"If the rules are too complicated, would a straightforward mapping work for the information?" Jennifer asked.

"That is how they do it now," Carl replied. "In the trial runs the users built a list of exceptions in a spreadsheet that they can use to fix the classifications that are not right."

"That sounds like that is the interim solution for this. Is there any reason at this stage that we need to do more than support the management and application of the mapping?" Jennifer asked.

"Not really, but it is not particularly master data," Carl mentioned.

"Unfortunately, in many cases the world does not always present us with perfect data scenarios where we can have the sacred single version of the truth. Our goal has to be to identify when this is the case and build the right solution," Jennifer said.

"So, what do we need to register in the mapping document for this?" Carl asked.

"We need to register that this is a specific mapping that is going to require a mapping table and then specify the shape of the mapping table that we need to build and implement. We should then add this to the backlog to be prioritised," Jennifer said.

"OK, I will do this. There are quite a few smaller mapping and classification tables that we need to store as part of the overall project; I will add these in the same way," Carl said.

"When you add them, can you add to the mapping sheet the expected frequency of maintenance or change for the mapping? It will help us to determine the appropriate solution for the implementation," Jennifer remarked.

"How do you want this stored?" Carl asked.

"Typically, these tables come in the form of:

- Static—Rarely changes.
- Infrequent—Changes but not very often. Classify these by the speed of change: monthly, annually, quarterly, weekly, etc.
- Per run—Every time the users need to produce an output.
- Transactional—Every transaction updates them or has the potential to.
- Realtime—It is consistently changing.

"Each of these will imply that we need to build a different solution," Jennifer added. "I will need all of these added into the mapping document ASAP, as I need to start looking at the backlog and working to get it prioritised."

"I can get this done by lunchtime tomorrow," Carl added.

"Have you got a list of all of the data quality issues that you have discovered in the data you have profiled?" Jennifer asked.

"Yes, we have been raising them like bugs in the software project. Dan asked us to put them onto the backlog under a specific category," Carl said.

"Great, that helps; I will look through those as well. We cannot assess the full scope until we know these wrinkles. Data is not so different to code in a system these days. The difference is that it changes based on user input and actions. You need to solve the conceptual shape of the data rather than the actual, in many cases by putting in specific patterns. What you have found will help me understand what needs to be done; we can then work on the who, what, and when of the solution," Jennifer said. "This is really helpful work that you and the team have done. It will help us to take some of the pressure off the IT team. Many of these issues are shared issues that we can work with the business to solve together," Jennifer said.

"Has Dan asked you to mock up a dataset using some sample feeds to iron out any other issues?" Jennifer continued.

"Yes, we are going to work with Ian's team to then run it past the business users to make sure we have captured the essence of what we are trying to do," Carl mentioned.

"Great, it should hopefully help with their engagement the more we can share of the direction that we are going in," Jennifer said.

They chatted on for a while longer before heading back to their desks. Jennifer spent some time acclimatising herself with the data quality issues, looking at the tickets raised, and adding it to the backlog that she was building of what needed to be done.

Her next meeting was with Justin Parkins, who would need to incorporate the new items and solutions into the architecture plans. That would be tomorrow morning, and today had been quite long, with the management meeting in the middle of the day and then the planning in the afternoon; it was time to switch off and start fresh tomorrow.

• • •

Jennifer was at her desk early. Her enthusiasm had taken a leap following the presentation yesterday, and her determination to succeed had grown with the need to demonstrate what could be done with the right approach. She was collating the logical pieces of the data steps that would be required to allow the users to work with the data. They had already identified two main data quality checks that needed to be fixed and several steps within the sign-off and report cycle that would require solutions. The meeting with Justin would be key to see if there were solutions in place or, at a minimum, placeholders. It would always be possible to do something in the interim and then refactor it later. However, she needed the team to have full knowledge of the scope from the outset, so that they would build the right framework for implementing a lasting solution.

They had booked coffee mid-morning to catch up. The coffee shop was a lot busier than it had been the night before. They sat at a table in the corner. Jennifer had her list of features that she was going to walk through with Justin.

"How has it been going?" Jennifer asked.

"We reviewed the solution that we worked on at the previous session. We have refactored the design to focus on producing reports and outputs from the central lake and the implementation of the reporting configurations closer to the users. The design is close to what we drew up in the last session," Justin said.

"Have you got a diagram to walk through?" Jennifer asked.

"Yes, I printed it off so we could look it over," Justin replied.

"Great. I have a list of items that Carl and his team have drawn together that we need to resolve and test the design against," Jennifer said.

Justin pulled the diagram from his folder and laid it out across the table. It was very similar to the diagram they had drawn up in the previous meeting.

"Here it is," he said. "I have incorporated the analytic builder component into the designs. The team have worked through the design of it and have established how it can be built. It will be optimised for pulling the bulk of the data from the lake. This will be based on a scoped query around the dataset that the user wants to retrieve.

"Given this, the queries will run quickly. The solution is scalable, since we have enabled it to have multiple threads that we will load balance against the resources that are available at any one point in time. The analytic sets will be built on the fly based on the size of the query, then they will be run with different levels of aggregation to make sure that the reporting tools are able to function correctly, even if the user requests too much data. We have added capabilities, as we discussed, to use the metadata to determine the amount of data in a query and to block requests that would consume too much resource. We think that this is achievable based on the technologies that we have available."

"That looks pretty good. Have you received the information from Carl on the types of data that they have and which sources to use?" Jennifer asked.

"I have; he mentioned yesterday that there is a little more that he is writing up and will get to us today," Justin replied.

"I have the list here in rough form; shall we walk it through on the architecture and then place the data types and volumes onto the architecture to see what the components are going to have to achieve?" Jennifer suggested.

They worked through the list of backlog items that Jennifer had with her from the previous day's discussions, and they started working through them one by one. Each one was established as a dataset here, and a flow there, a maintenance screen there.

"Where should we put the logic and the data?" Justin asked.

"The key is to put the data with the highest velocity of change as close to the users as possible. This will enable us to then keep up with the speed of change that they implement," Jennifer replied.

"What if it is shared across multiple requirements?" Justin asked.

"We need to put it in a shared dataset that can be picked up by multiple analytic set builders. This is the reason we need to make sure that the data does not get embedded into the reporting process. If it is, then we will end up with having duplicate logic across reports, which either slows down future changes or means that over time the logic drifts apart and the versions of the truth start to diverge," Jennifer explained.

The pair of them verified the components and the data within the architecture, established the workloads for each of the components, and described the features and functions in terms of data in and out and how to handle the logic. In most cases they tried to get the logic to be defined with the data rather than creating business logic–specific coded modules that would require release.

"I understand what we need to do," Justin said. "It is more work than we had planned in the timeline," he mentioned.

"Can we add the work to the backlog that we have? Then we can work out the priority to get this implemented and then decide what is required in the first implementation and what can be a tactical solution," Jennifer said.

They worked through and established the backlog of changes that would need to be made to achieve the solution. They then started to assign estimates on the work to implement the tasks and assign them to the plan.

"If we implement all of this, then either we need ten more resources, or we need to delay the go live for another three to six months," Justin said.

"I expected that," Jennifer said calmly. "Let's go through and prioritise the work that definitely needs to be an IT solution in the first instance."

"OK, that comes out as being achievable, with some time to spare," Justin said.

"Next let's prioritise the other items into things that either we can do to put in place an interim solution, or we can put a manual procedure in place for," Jennifer said.

They worked through the items, most of which were related to the maintenance of items that would support the specific reports. These were the additional items that represented the work that the users historically were doing outside of the official systems.

"The problem is that all of the work that gets added due to the new analysis has caused the overrun," Justin said.

"This is what I thought would happen," Jennifer said. "What we need to do now is to make sure that this extra work is implemented with the right structure, even if it needs to be implemented by the users in the short term. That way we can then make it easy for us to work through and slowly add into the future platform. What fallback options can we implement to meet the deadline based on this information?" she asked.

Justin thought for a while. "Some of this data is hardly changing at all. Some mappings here, some lookups, and some classifications. In the interim we can add these into the solution as files without the means to update them and then create manual procedures for updating them," Justin said. "Some of the other items in the list we can implement in a couple of ways to form a stop gap until we can get a strategic component into the hole."

They worked through the items on the plan, adding in the compromises and then adding tasks into the backlog with the appropriate notes. The plan looked like it could run. It included the right shape for the job, and it would enable them to build upon it by implementing better components in the future.

"It is still coming out too long. At the beginning of the plan, there is this large dependency in the plan that means that the reporting team cannot start work until the data is available from the calculations. This is pushing us over the deadline," Justin observed.

"Yes, this is typical of data projects. The end of the pipeline must always wait for the front of the pipeline to succeed before it can start implementation. This is what always forces these projects into waterfall," Jennifer explained. "Is there a way you can see in the plan to break the dependency?" she asked.

"The one place that we can break the dependency is the interface between calculation output and the reporting layer. This is defined by the shape of the data that we are implementing in the data lake," Justin said.

"Can we somehow use this as a synchronisation point, which we can then use as the point of integration between the two halves of the project?" Jennifer asked.

"We can do that. If we define the schema that is written down onto disk, then we can put some test data into the schema to enable the reporting layer to run with, and then that team can work with the users to get the design implemented," Justin said.

"That will work—we can use the analyst team to generate some mock data for the reporting layer to enable them to move forwards," Jennifer said. "Looking at the plans, if we can use the schema to break this dependency, then we will still be able to hit the deadline. The additional risk is that the calculation team cannot meet this schema," Jennifer said.

"I don't think that will be a major issue. Most of the risk calculations follow a similar schema from the overnight risk runs. This has always been the case. We know this pretty well based on what we have implemented in the past," Justin said.

"I know, but it is still a risk, and we should add it to the risk log," Jennifer explained. "We should get the priority of the data model to the top of the list and get Dan, Carl, and the team to start work on this ASAP."

Jennifer and Justin really liked the plan. This would enable them to crash the critical path and run streams in parallel. It is not typical of how projects are run, but then data projects are not like other projects. The pipeline is long and contains many places where dependencies can get it clogged up. The trick is always to loosen the dependencies without breaking coherence and adding reconciliations, checks, and balances. The balance is made even harder by the requirement for data projects to be agile and adaptable to meet the needs of the users.

The project plan broke down nicely into organised teams that would be small enough to make rapid progress and focused enough to minimise the amount of cross-team communication. Jennifer and Justin put together the tasks and the effort to form a presentation to enable her to share it with the stakeholders. She could now spend the day tidying it up and sharing it with the individuals who needed to buy into the plans.

Her meeting with Brian was tomorrow. She was going to prepare the required functional requirements of the system alongside the plan. The deadline would not enable them to implement everything perfectly in the first iteration. To progress this, she would need to get approval for the overall structure and framework and then the components and the compromises. Alongside the compromise she would present the future target. Brian could then indicate if she had compromised in the right places.

If Brian approved of the plan, then they would need to focus on the interface and the layout of the system, and they would need to model the flow of the data. They would have to process billions of rows of data for each run, and getting logic in the wrong place would cause the whole flow to bottleneck. They would need to take the data captured by Carl and his team and run it through the calculations. This could wait until the overall approach was approved.

• • •

Jennifer's regular meeting with Brian was bright and early, straight after the regular global call. Brian was his usual energetic self, warm and friendly to Jennifer when she arrived.

"Hi, Brian, I hope that you are well. Did you see the changes to the regulatory submission introduced last week?" Jennifer asked.

"Yes, it seems that they want to capture a bit more detail than previously asked. It is not a lot different, just a couple of formats and groupings of risk. It seems the further they get through the project, the more they realise what is possible and what is not based on feedback from the firms that are contributing. I know we have been lobbying with them hard based on what we can produce. Flexibility is key!" Brian said.

"Very true, isn't it always? I wanted to walk through the plans for Aspen with you. We have broken down the work remaining, and, thanks to the additional information provided by your team, we have a more complete solution. I was going to walk through this to get your input on the required features and then the plan and the compromises," Jennifer said.

"OK, thanks," said Brian.

"Here is the list of the original tasks that were identified by the BRD process. We have now identified these additional tasks relating to the user interaction and the requirement to cleanse and conform the data. As you can see, there are several steps here that are currently being done outside the data system for the purpose of producing the output. If we want people to use Aspen, we need to add these into the overall flow," Jennifer explained. They walked through the individual mappings, lookups, and classifications, and Brian gave his input on each one. They managed to eliminate a couple of tasks, but overall, it described the full workflow.

"What is the damage?" Brian asked.

"The additional work would take us over the deadline," Jennifer said. "However, working with Justin, we think we are able to split the team in two and focus one subteam on building the user interaction and the other on generating the calculations," Jennifer said.

Brian considered this. "Normally the business teams work better when they have numbers," Brian mentioned.

"We will give them numbers through an extract from the calculation run. We will then use old numbers or mocked-up numbers within the interface. It will enable both teams to move much faster. The generation of the numbers is moving at the speed of the risk generators, which is not fast enough for the work that needs to be done in the reporting and sign-off layer," Jennifer said.

"OK, I think that can work for us," Brian said. "What else is there?"

"We need to find some compromises on the solution for go live that need to move to being implemented strategically after the deadline. Currently, the users create several mappings that enable them to filter and classify the risk correctly. We would like them to continue to do this off the main systems and then send us the mappings. We will create manual procedures to add these into the system. Normally, we would build maintenance screens, but we do not have time," Jennifer asked.

"Sounds reasonable; are you going to be able to do this with the change mechanisms?" Brian asked.

"I am going to ask for exceptions. They are relatively slow moving, so we can make something work," Jennifer said.

"OK, let me know if you need some help," Brian said.

They carried on working through the logistics of the plan, with Brian identifying point people to focus on the streams. Overall, he was happy with the process.

Jennifer returned to her office, wanting to put the plans into a presentable form. If she were to win the support for putting in manual procedures, she would need to get the support of Mark and Gary Jeffersen. She was feeling more confident in the planning. The solution would meet the needs of the users, and the planning approach would enable them to build momentum and to reduce dependencies. This would enable the team to work in an agile way, which was crucial for the development team to interact effectively with the users.

Jennifer's next focus would be on making sure that the architecture would support the vision and enable them to iterate and extend the components without having to completely reengineer the whole solution for every new requirement.

Closing Questions

The key to DataOps is to be able to build solutions rapidly, seeking feedback and in some cases failing fast to later come up with the right solution. This is achieved by organising data and processes correctly. Here are some questions to ask yourself:

- When you're requested to make a change to the system, does that change get queued up with many other changes and take a long time to release?
- Are your users constantly unhappy with the speed to change the system?
- Is there a way you can show results early?
- Do you struggle to break down plans into trackable iterations?
- Is there a way to establish a test-driven continuous integration approach to the components of your data and analytics solution?

Chapter 8

Setting Up the Framework

Key Concepts

To grow upwards, you need the right foundations. You need the right patterns and shapes to enable you to add the structure on top and to continue to build upwards to reach new heights. In data solutions, there are a set of frameworks and foundations that need to be built. Building an infrastructure footprint and installing the right technologies on it to accept data used to be one of the critical-path elements in the timeline of your solution. This is changing gradually, as data solutions and infrastructure move to the cloud and can be scripted in much the same way as your code.

However, being able to leverage the cloud, the right components and the right glue between components takes time. Often tactical solutions can be put in place to carry out a functional workload of the system; despite this, every effort should be made further down the delivery path to refactor the tactical solution to build it into a strategic component. Data is acting more and more like code within a data and analytics system. In the successful systems we have built, treating the data model like libraries of code that can be added into a build script to support new analysis rapidly has been key to building the flexibility to survive the passage of time. Often requirements can change at the last minute, and having to rewire the whole data architecture to support this will take too long. Avoiding hard coding of relationships and embedding local variables at the global level helps you to avoid many of these pitfalls.

J ENNIFER SPENT the rest of the day preparing the communications to Mark and Gary. What she was planning in the short term would cause her to be frowned upon by the quality standards that existed within IT. Changing data via change control would mean that there was a recognised risk that the data could be tampered with on its way through the system.

The interesting irony in this was that by not doing this she would have to continue allowing the users to process the data downstream. Her philosophy was better the devil you know than the devil you do not. By having visibility of the manual procedures, the IT team would be able to understand what they were and to schedule remediation. Allowing the users to implement their tools would mean the investment in Aspen would be to calculate and store numbers that would eventually become obsolete due to the lack of attention. It was a fine balance.

She put together a best estimate of the effort involved to remediate the manual procedures, and she worked out what would be a reasonable schedule to do so under the likely post-release bulge in activity. The communication was put forward, strongly making the following positive points:

- The key benefit was the fact that post release the users would be working within the IT system rather than outside.
- The manual processes would be remediated rapidly. She had scheduled three months post release, with a couple of interim releases to remove most of the procedures.

Given the urgency, she scheduled a meeting for the following day to walk through the plans with Mark and Gary. She would spend the rest of the day putting together a schedule of meetings to be able to agree upon the scalable architecture and approach. With two separate teams working independently, it would be important for them to understand in detail the interface between them. She was also keen to make sure that the platform built would be extensible to meet the future needs. This would involve clever modelling, clever organisation of processes, and the ability to dynamically update the architecture to support the future needs with minimal rework.

• • •

The meeting with Mark and Gary had been squeezed into the early morning. Normally their diaries were difficult to get in, so Jennifer was pleased for the exception.

"Hi, thank you for taking this meeting at short notice. I appreciate that your busy schedules would have made this hard to fit in. I have been working with the team on the plan for Aspen. On new analysis, the BRD is missing a key component of the application that we need to make sure that the platform achieves the outcomes that you and I want from the project," Jennifer stated.

She walked through the missing features in the design and explained how they were being achieved currently and the vision for the future.

"The challenge that I have is the looming deadline," she continued. "Given this vision, there is not enough time to put robust components in place for all of the user interactions. To address this, we have split the plan to free up more time, which will enable us to run both streams—reporting and generation—at full velocity. This gives us a lot of time back and enables us to complete many of the new items; however, it is likely that there will need to be some manual updates in place of user interfaces to support the full workflow. Here are the items and the expected speed of update, and here is the schedule for replacing them post release." Jennifer presented the datasets that needed to be maintained manually alongside the speed with which they were estimated to change. "I am asking for permission to manually update these feeds through change procedure for an interim period post initial release," she completed.

"When you say interim period, how long do you expect it to go on for, and how often are you expecting the data to be updated?" Gary asked.

"The data we are looking to update is in this table," Jennifer explained, bringing up the table with the list of manual processes on the screen. "Each of the entities are described, and the purpose for them is explained. The expected update frequency is in the table. Most refinements of the data are for the reporting system and happen for every iteration of the calculation. Given how the users work, this tends to be twice a week maximum," Jennifer explained.

"I would see that increasing as we reach the deadline," Mark said.

"I agree; as the final report is being refined, I would expect that the frequency will increase. There is a physical constraint on how fast they can iterate due to the time it takes to run a risk calculation," Jennifer explained.

"The problem that we have is that we are measured on the churn of the systems. This is down to the risk that if things are changing too quickly, then it is perceived that the system is unstable or, worse, it is being manipulated. With all the recent issues with rogue traders, the bank is tight on these things. Therefore, there is a dashboard that we produce for senior management that I need to explain. This will push some of the metrics through thresholds," Mark said.

"That is the reason for this meeting. We need to reason with management to ask if this can be an exception in the short term, knowing that this will mean the overall success of the system in the longer term," Jennifer noted.

"The problem that we could have is that the users do not sponsor the improvements to the system that allow this to go away in the timeframes that we want. They always want the next thing. We will need Brian's word that he will support the work required to sort this out," Gary said.

"I have spoken to Brian already, and he has indicated that he is happy to support the remediation work post release. He is supportive of the plan. I walked him through the vision of the completed system, and he was supportive of the overall solution," Jennifer explained.

"That is good, because it is going to take both of us to talk to management to be able to get an exception passed. I am supportive of your plans, as it is the right thing to do; however, we do need to sort out the impression this is going to give through senior management, who also need to demonstrate that our systems are controlled and supported," Mark said.

"Thank you, Mark, what do you need from me to help with this?" Jennifer asked.

"Can you forward me a one-page explanation of the plans, explaining why they are necessary, what the end goal is, how we will have controls in place to make sure this does not go on for long and that the manually entered data has checks and balances in place?" Mark asked.

Jennifer thought it somewhat ironic that to build an IT system to support and control that was already happening would take so much explanation to the powers that be. It was clear they were happier with things happening outside of what they knew.

"I can do that," Jennifer said. "I will get the information to you by midmorning. Do you want to set up a call with Brian to make sure that we are all in agreement on the need to remediate this quickly?" Jennifer asked.

"No, I will give him a call this morning to square this off," Mark said.

"I will make the change board aware of this coming and make sure that we are able to handle what is needed," Gary said.

"Thank you," Jennifer replied.

They quickly concluded the meeting and got on with the task of setting up the exception processes.

Jennifer hurried back to her desk and quickly put together the information that Gary and Mark required. She had achieved what she needed. Now she needed to focus on the framework with the team.

• • •

Jennifer knew that the key to the success of the team over the long term was to make the framework extensible. She had already provided some steer to Justin around making sure that the solution could quickly respond to the needs of the users for reporting. She would now need to focus to build the right shape for the foundations.

She needed to spend some time looking at the way the solution was working from calculations to storage. It seemed to be that the work done was putting data into the lake efficiently, but once it was there, they had very limited reuse. Each project was having to write the data again, causing duplication of common entities and therefore inconsistencies. The hope of having one version of the truth was sadly not happening. Jennifer spent the next couple of hours reviewing the data that was being stored in the lake—the format, the shape, and to some extent the technologies chosen. She understood what the team were doing and how they were representing the data, but she did not really know why they had chosen to do it this way.

She called Justin to ask. "Hi, Justin, have you got a minute to take me through the data ingestion to the system?"

Justin arrived in her office with John Foster. "Hi, Jennifer, you know John from our team meetings. He is taking the lead on the data generation. He has been a key member of the team for the past couple of years," Justin said.

"Hi, John, nice to meet you. I have heard a lot about the work you have been doing," Jennifer said. "I was just reviewing the models that store the data for the risk calculations for the Aspen project. I notice that they are completely new for this project in comparison to Vermont. Is there a reason for this?" Jennifer asked.

"The requirements for the projects were different for Aspen in comparison to Vermont. The scenarios for the risk calculations are completely different, meaning that we could not use the same data format," John said.

"You're right, the scenarios are different; however, they are described by the scenario engine, which means they have a consistent definition structure," Jennifer said.

"The data needs to be stored down with this definition, and the shape of it is different to Vermont. The calculations generating the numbers are different," John said.

"So, we are storing the definition of the calculation alongside the numbers?" Jennifer asked.

"Yes, that way the consuming applications know what it is they are consuming, which enables them to work faster," John said.

"What happens when the regulator asks for a new calculation?" Jennifer asked.

"We would need to look at it and then potentially write a new set of data files to the system," John said. "This is totally fine because of the flexibility we have writing to file system rather than database tables. Everything becomes self-describing, which really speeds up the time to ingest data. We then use schema on read to work out how to serve it up. We have tools to make this quicker," John said.

"Reading this back, there is very little consistency in the data structures used across different projects?" Jennifer asked. "We are also storing all the descriptive data alongside the calculations?"

"Yes, it is the new way. Metadata describes the data, meaning that you can ingest quickly," John said.

"So, the complexity is deferred to later?" Jennifer said.

"Yes, schema on read and the power of the lake gives us this flexibility," John said.

Jennifer was starting to get concerned. The shape of risk was pretty much consistent across all the calculations. The dimensionality of the numbers subtly changed based on asset class and risk type, but broadly these were a finite number of patterns. By storing the data like this, they were saving problems for later down the line. In addition, the files were very large. This meant that they were becoming too large to manipulate effectively.

"Where does the business logic go in the designs at the moment?" Jennifer asked.

"In the Vermont project we built an API for the users, and we built a set of reports that produced the target output. We designed a nice HTML5 interface for the reports. Each one formatted to the specification," John replied.

"Was the business logic contained in the reading process and duplicated in the front end and the API?" Jennifer asked.

"Some of it we reused; however, the queries were particular, so we coded up logic to read it and format it for the requirement," John said.

Jennifer had seen this before and found that the outcome was symptomatic of the BRD process. The contract that was supposed to communicate the solution was constraining the output due to its tick box nature. The management of data did not typically work in this way, because the reports were only a small part of the story. She would have to find a way to steer the team to a different approach. She had already separated the concerns by splitting the teams and using a consistent data model as the integration point. The key now was to make sure that the nuances in the schema were separated appropriately in the design. This would be defined by the modelling work that Dan Churchill and Carl Hinckley were doing.

"Due to the deadline that we have, and the need to meet it to satisfy the regulator, we have separated data production from data and analytics. We are going to have to decide on a consistent format to integrate the two halves together. This format needs to satisfy the requirements of the data production team and the needs of the reporting team. It should be flexible enough to support future implementations without the need for a new schema," Jennifer stated.

"In my experience," she continued, "a lot of the core data is consistent between projects. We need to extract that and start to identify what is not consistent and then work out the best way to manage it. The core schema will act as the anchor to hold the solution together. We can split it up based on subjects and topics to make the modelling and the organisation of it simpler. We can use the scope information being captured by Carl and Dan to identify the requirement-specific data, which we need to append to the core schema in a flexible and consistent way. The data model and how it is implemented is going to be key to the solution's working effectively. We will need to use some extensible modelling techniques to enable us to limit the dependencies between generation and consumption," Jennifer said.

"It sounds like we need to add some logic into the ingestion to make the data map to a consistent schema," John said.

"Yes, I agree, most of the core data should be consistent anyway. We need to quickly arrive at the right model, as this is on the critical path for hitting the deadline," Jennifer said. "Dan and Carl have done analysis on this in the mapping sheets, and we are going to work on how this can be supported," Jennifer replied.

"We will need to calculate the work required to do this, as we have made plans based on reusing our existing ingestion engines," John said.

"Of course, we may not get there in one jump, but I want to define the shape of what we are aiming for before we go too far," Jennifer said. "I will set up a session to work through the interface with Dan and Carl."

"OK," John said.

"Can you include myself and Harry Isles? He is leading the reporting side in this," Justin asked.

"Yes, of course, we need to all 'buy in' to the way forwards to make a success of this," Jennifer replied.

"If we go with a standardised schema, won't we just create a big bottleneck around its implementation?" John asked.

"This is where we need to focus on extensible schemas and to make sure that the schema can be extended in a controlled way," Jennifer said.

"How can we do that given the fact that as soon as we build it, we are going to end up with downstream processes being highly dependent on the schema?" John asked.

"There are some patterns that we can employ that will enable us to extend the schema in an incremental way. We can use these patterns to create a loosely coupled extensible schema that enables us to make changes incrementally," Jennifer said.

"What happens when the user asks for something new?" John said.

"That is the secret; typically users ask one of two things:

1. A new calculation, in which case, with a good design of the core schema, we should be able to add the new calculation incrementally without schema change; or

2. A new grouping, or post-process calculation, in which case this happens much closer to the reporting system, so that the work that the production team are doing is not impacted.

"If the schema is constantly changing, then we have got something wrong," Jennifer continued.

"If we implement reference data separate to calculation, it would mean lots of joins to the data downstream of the storage layer!" John said.

"Joins are necessary and post-storage calculations are necessary to configure the right reporting in the system," Jennifer replied.

"The reason we have not done this is that the lake is much more efficient at running queries on big tables," John said.

"I know, that is why we need to consider which parts the lake handles and which part is handled by other technologies in a post process. We need to be using technologies appropriately for what they are good at. The requirements definition is consistent and does not care about what the lake can and cannot do, so we may need to look at alternatives," Jennifer said.

John was looking a little fed up. Although they had achieved a lot with the solution to date, it was not working efficiently to enable them to hit this new deadline. Jennifer would have to tread carefully to make sure that he could change his perspective and buy into a new way to organise the solution.

To move John's thinking forward, the three of them sat down and walked through the design of the end solution, step by step. They worked through what existed and what would need to be done to implement a different design and meet the deadline. At the end of the session John was starting to come around. He could see the way that the overall architecture could be implemented to work to the strengths of the technology that they had available.

The three of them concluded that the key meeting was to pull the team together and decide on the schema that would provide the integration point for the project. Jennifer took the action to set the meeting up in the diary, and Justin and John left Jennifer's office.

On reflection of the meeting with John, Jennifer realised the importance of defining effective data models. Up to this point the team had been hard coding relationships into the Big Data file structures. This was causing them to have to write new data for each requirement. IT management had sold the fact that they had populated the data lake with lots of data. This was OK, but the business could not consume it effectively, and it was difficult to link it back to business process. They had therefore used the lake as staging data for processes that they then built into end-user solutions outside of governance and control.

Jennifer sat at her desk looking for a time slot for the data modelling meeting, which would become crucial for the project team, and saw that 10 AM tomorrow was free for most. She set up the meeting with key people in attendance. They needed to move fast, and there was only enough time to bring the leaders on the journey. They could then filter the outcome down to their teams. Carl Hinckley and Dan Churchill would represent data analysis and modelling; Justin Parkins, Harry Isles, and John Foster were key to the technology teams; and Ian Cole would represent the business analysts.

Once the invite was sent, she spent a few hours with Dan preparing for the meeting. They would need to use all their experience to be able to move the team forwards. Given the time pressures, it would take quite a direct approach at this stage to instigate the change that would be required. Once people were on the right track, she would be able to be more facilitative in her approach. They broke the meeting down into five sections:

1. The problem statements
2. The high-level solution architecture
3. The desired outcomes
4. Defining the model for integration
5. Identifying work, risks, and issues

Most of the time would be spent on defining the integration model, but this needed to be set up with everyone working from the same base understanding of the problem statements, architecture, and vision.

The meeting was planned for most of the day. The goal for the meeting was to come out with the model and the technologies agreed. This would need a clear understanding of the requirements aligned to the capabilities of the tools. The work that Dan and Carl had done would clearly define the size of the data. The work that Ian and his team had completed clearly defined different views on the data that they needed to support. Dan felt confident that he understood the data well enough to be able to place it into the right scope.

Jennifer and Dan worked late into the evening before heading home to get some rest, feeling happy that they had produced what they needed to work through the meeting successfully.

• • •

The following day Jennifer and Dan got to the meeting room early and spent time setting up all the materials on the display to enable them to walk through the information logically. Everyone arrived to the meeting on time, grabbed refreshments, and sat down. Jennifer introduced the meeting and ran through the problem statement.

"Hi everyone, thank you for coming to the meeting. We are here to put together the interface between the consuming team led by Harry, who will be working and iterating with the users on the risk reporting, and the production team led by John, who will be working on generating, refining, and persisting the risk results. The teams are led by Justin Parkins, who is responsible for the overall technology delivery.

"The importance of splitting into two teams is to run both teams in parallel to be able to hit the deadline in front of us. The benefit of doing this is that the teams can break dependencies and work at their own velocities. In separating into two teams, we should be able to stay on track and deliver what the users need. This is not a normal situation. This method of delivery increases integration risk; however, we plan to mitigate that by having a clearly defined interface," Jennifer said.

They worked through the problem statement in greater detail, with Ian taking the lead from the user requirements perspective. Justin then walked through the solution architecture that he had drawn up, and Carl presented the data that they had collated to support the project.

"Is everyone happy with the requirements and how we are going to build the project?" Jennifer asked. "Has anyone got any questions?" They had thoroughly covered the materials, and everyone was happy to move on.

Jennifer started the next agenda item—the integration model. "When we put together the model, we need to consider the following criteria:

1. It needs to be extensible. We need to be able to extend it without having to go through lengthy regression testing.
2. It needs to be scalable. It needs to support greater volumes, because we do not fully know what the users want next.
3. We need to make it reusable. By pulling out consistent shapes, we want those shapes to support future models.
4. We want it to support high performance. It needs to be able to react to changing needs and run quickly enough to support reruns.
5. It needs to support instrumentation and quality checks. We do not want errors propagating through the system unchecked, requiring us to go through lengthy unwind procedures.

"I have added Dan Churchill to this team to aid with the modelling effort. Dan has worked on implementing a similar approach on our previous project, where we established a model for supporting these principles," Jennifer concluded.

Dan took centre stage, bringing up the data sheet on the screen. "I have been working with Carl Hinckley on the data analysis. We have built up a spreadsheet of the data that we need to support the Aspen requirements. This has been put together in the sheet I am showing on the screen. We have categorised the information in the following ways:

1. Subject: What is the key entity that the data is associated with?
2. Volatility: How often is the data changing?
3. Size: How large are the data fields and how many rows of each entity do we expect?
4. What are the primary key and business key?
5. Type: Is it a classification, or hierarchy, or fact, or dimension, etc.?
6. Scope: How wide is this variable scoped to the report, process, department, organisation, etc.?

"This information will help us to place the information correctly onto the data model and determine how we manage the data. On a separate sheet we have mapped this information back to the source of where we expect to get it from. We have spent time checking these sources and then making sure all of the data from source is consistent with the information in the sheet." Dan walked through the mapping sheets as he was talking.

"As a second exercise, we have profiled the source data, and we have identified data quality issues. This has led to the requirement for additional mapping tables that we will need to cleanse the information from source," Dan continued.

"We have added to this a day in the life of the system to identify the timing of the data pipeline against the SLAs and to understand any dependency issues." Dan showed the day in the life of the system. All the information presented gave them everything they needed to understand the data flow to support the Aspen requirement.

Dan then took the workings from the data sheet and presented a conceptual view of the data. "On this next sheet we have taken a conceptual view of the entities and have grouped them by their subject, by the type of the data, and by their scope. This gives us a logical layout of where data needs to be introduced into the pipeline. We have applied the logical rule that we want to join as late as possible whilst maintaining integrity throughout."

"Why have you done that?" John asked.

"The reason to do this is that hard coding things early in the pipeline forces you to have to test everything downstream every time the users want a change. By introducing data as late as possible, then there is less to test and therefore greater flexibility in the system," Dan said.

"That is not what makes the lake efficient. It is OK with a few simple joins on select. We build big tables to then enable the users to have lots of dimensionality in their queries," John said.

"This does represent a change in approach," Dan said. "Storing less hard-coded join information in the data gives us flexibility to iterate the interface layer with the users. This will make us more dynamic and more agile. In addition, hard coding relationships early in the data model makes the data structures and the pipeline less reusable. When additional requirements are added for the same data, but with slight variations, the options are to create a new table and have no reuse, or to add additional columns to the existing table. This is not sustainable over the long term and leads to the project getting stuck," Dan said.

"How will you overcome the performance issues of the joins?" John asked.

"The challenge is that the lake is good for large search criteria over a large dataset. As you mention, it is not good for joining lots of data together. That is why we will be storing some of these relationship tables outside of the lake and then joining them downstream to build reporting and analytics sets for the users to use. If the users change their minds on the relationship, then we can change it quickly with this design and present the new data to them. It does not take a full rebuild of the data that we have stored," Dan said.

"How are we going to store the data then?" John asked.

"That is what we are here to resolve. There is not a single correct answer to this question that works for every use case past, present, and future. There is just a set of principles to follow and several theories that exist to guide us. The principles that have worked for me in the past are:

- Pass by reference. Establish unique keys consistently based on subject and then use them throughout the pipeline. This has the benefit of making it possible to look up data based on the key at whatever point you want without having to carry hard-coded values through the pipeline.
- Join as late as possible and as close to the reporting or end output as possible. This provides you with the ability to change things rapidly when people want to see new perspectives on the data.
- Enable extension to the schema. This can be achieved to enable individual sandbox data and is a life saver if you need to patch something in quickly. Our job is to empower this innovation in a controlled and governed way.
- Store versions of the data that you have. Be careful not to delete detail too early. Otherwise, if it is needed later you will have a lot of work to do. Think of building a report as the steps in linking compiled modules of code together. Rather than it being code, it is compiled datasets and entities. Our job is to design the entities as reusable packages with embedded quality and metadata to enable people to pull them together for new requirements.
- Store data with different scopes in the right place. Think of some data as state, some data as local variables, and some as global variables. Ideally, you

are trying to make things as consistent as possible globally; however, this has the negative impact of introducing side effects and large testing cycles. Having everything as local variables creates duplication and leads to inconsistencies and drift between the applications."

"Are there any questions about these principles?" Dan asked.

"The problem is that they are not particularly clear cut," John said.

"You are right, that is why we need to balance the design based on the information that Ian and Carl have collected and our combined knowledge of what 'good' looks like. The challenge that we have and the reason for a data model design is to make the appropriate compromises that avoid issues in the future. This enables us to remain agile and responsive," Dan answered.

"Here are some of the other principles that had helped me in the past:

- Firstly, avoid unnecessary translation. When data is written in one shape, do not translate it through different schemas unless necessary. The reason for this is:
    - It is inefficient.
    - You lose the meaning of the original data.
    - You force people to comply with a schema that few people understand.
    - You get bottlenecked around data modelers.
- It is OK to have a semantic schema to aid understanding. This is used in many places for defining common terms and meanings; however, this should not represent the physical schema. The physical schema should aid the delivery of data to where it is needed and map to the logical schema for understanding.
- Expect that relationships in a system will grow and change. It is our ability to support this flexibility that enables insight to be built with the data. Forming relationships is the key to gaining actionable knowledge in data science," Dan finished.

"How do we do this?" John asked.

"These are the steps that I follow:

- Categorise by scope—Establish for each field what it is and if it is core or dressing.
- Group by subject—Subjects are defined by what the data relates to. For example, is it information about a customer, or a security, or an internal organisation?
- Break out into types—Is it a fact, a relationship, a time-constrained value, or workflow state?
- Establish supporting tables—Category, groupings, and hierarchy tables.
- Look at the grain—Establish the grain of the data.

- Look at the flow—Where does the data need to be added, how does it need to be stored? What is the source and what is the workflow, how will it be queried, and what capacity is needed?
- Map the schema onto the physical model—We will likely have different tools for different jobs—i.e., relational / semi structured for ref data, tables for facts, graphs for relationships, unstructured for logs and context information.
- Finalise the interface—The outcome is the persistent interface between producers and consumers.
- Test against the requirements—Check that the required datasets can be generated.

"From the work that Carl and I have been doing, we have already completed the scope and subject classification, so I propose to walk through it and then establish the core schema.* We can also walk through all the schemas that we need to generate to support the user interface and the requirements," Dan finished.

The team walked through the data requirements and the data in mapping spreadsheets captured by Carl and Dan. The information contained in the sheets made it easy to map the information onto the steps they were taking. By removing the joins from the schema at the beginning, it was then much easier to model the core components. By working to the rules and the principles, it was easy to get the data flow mapped. The resulting core schema represented a schema that was consistent across many use cases, and then the supporting tables were simple to establish. Data from the profiling helped them to structure the data flow and highlight where additional mappings would be needed.

They tested the schema against the requirements to check that it would support new features efficiently and effectively. They could add new risk scenarios easily for most of the cases that they could imagine. At the end of the process,

---

* The purpose of this book is not to go into detailed modelling methods. That has been done in these books: *The Data Warehouse Toolkit* by Kimball and Ross [Wiley. ISBN: 9781118530801]; and *Building a Scalable Data Warehouse with Data Vault 2.0* by Linstedt and Olschimke [Morgan Kaufmann. ISBN: 9780128026489]. The key here is to pull out the methodology that is different due to the DataOps approach. This is based around reusable, extensible schemas. Categorisation of data and the reduction of dependencies through the pipeline are the key elements that are missing from most modelling approaches. These enable you to remain dynamic and efficient. In each use case, risk modelling, customer analytics modelling, P&L MIS, etc., schemas will be different based on the requirements and the data flow specific to the problem. Therefore, focusing on an outcome-driven approach and following the DataOps principles are the key to getting it right.

they had a schema and data flow that could be used to support the interface between producing and consuming. The tables that were required to iterate reporting were in the hands of the consumers and would enable them to provide many perspectives without needing to change the main flow of data.

"This has been a really good exercise," Justin said. "I think we have a way forwards that will enable us to continue to move efficiently and effectively. John and Harry, are you able to work with this?"

"Yes, but it gives us a lot less to focus on," John said.

"I think that due to the deadline, the only way that we can get the work done in time is by getting the core data clean and in a state to be used by the consumers," Justin replied.

"I guess so; we should, numbers permitting, be able to support this," John said.

"I like it," Harry replied. "With this level of empowerment from organising the data, we will be able to engage with the users to meet their needs!"

"That sounds good," Justin replied.

"We can mock up some data for you to represent the requirements while you are waiting on the data production to come through," Carl added. "That way you should be able to start the iterations with the users immediately."

"Great," Harry said.

"We have all the models and the datasets established, which is great. Can we get these written up and sent around for review? Secondly, based on this, please can you reorganise your sprint plans to incorporate the work?" Jennifer asked.

The meeting tailed off. There was much more energy coming from the teams, as they felt that destiny was back in their own hands.

The teams returned to their desks. Justin took on the role to write up the models and the flow of the data to send around to the teams. Carl and Dan took the responsibility to update the mapping documents and to add the shape of the data in the new models. John and Harry took responsibility to reorganise their sprint plans and backlogs. They had agreed to get this together in two days, with a plan to regroup at the end of the week. They would need to communicate the plans and then start to shape the implementation. Key to this would be the new flow of the data and the size and shape of it. The technologies that they were planning to use would need to be checked and thought through.

Closing Questions

The foundations of DataOps need to be in place to enable the DevOps-style delivery pipeline for your data projects. Here are some questions to ask yourself:

- Does your data and analytics pipeline contain many black boxes that lack transparency and create side effects?
- Have you hardcoded any of your data logic?
- At what stage are you building your datasets?
- Do you struggle to get your first delivery out to the users within a short timeframe?
- Are you able to create a set of discrete components that can be leveraged, reused, and tested independently?

Chapter 9

Technology Choice

Key Concepts

Design is a series of compromises that you must make to balance functionality, performance, and cost. The challenge of a team designing a system is to define the problem in a scientific way and to have an eye to the future to make sure that you are making the compromises in the right places. Often storage can be traded for performance—by making joins early in the pipeline, you are trading the performance of the ingestion and standardisation for the performance and processing requirements of the query. By building a schema on read system, you are trading understanding the data at the start of the project to understanding it on consumption.

Understanding the types of data that you are manipulating and their usage within the data pipeline can help you architect the best way to store them. Typically, facts are happy being stored in large, partitioned tables, whilst reference data is happier in relational or object-based storage. The key is to have a good definition of the usage of the data and the non-functional requirements so that you can design the system to meet expectations and push back where those expectations are unreasonable. The work that you do to build up a data-driven picture of the requirement and the underlying data will support you in making these correct choices.

T HE END of the week came around quickly, and they had published the data model that would form the glue within the system. They went about collating all the information that they would need for the design of the system. Through the process of using the metadata and fitting it to the data model and the data flow, they were able to draw up accurate definitions of what the structure of the data architecture needed to be and the specifications of the individual components within it. They all met inside the main IT conference room with the documents to support their data architecture decisions. Justin took the lead in the meeting.

"Hi everyone; it has been a busy week, but I feel we have made a lot of progress in building consensus on the data architecture. I have brought before and after pictures to highlight where the differences have been made," Justin said. He brought up a data flow diagram onto the screen showing the way they were processing the data originally in Aspen (see Figure 9.1).

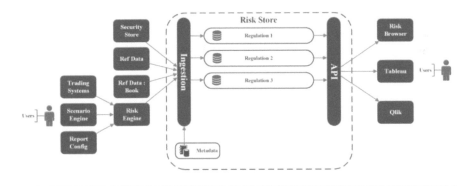

Figure 9.1   Justin's architecture diagram for the old way of processing the risk.

"Here you can see us consuming data from the upstream calculators and then storing it in the Big Data platforms. For efficiency, we stored it in big tables with relationships added to the files so that the query engine would be able to process the data and serve it up to the users," Justin continued.

"Based on the analysis that Carl and Dan have completed, I have been able to size the data in the system for the Aspen runtime requirement." Justin brought up the sizes in rows and columns of the big tables and the sum of the rows and the columns. "For a single report in the regulatory submission, we process and generate twenty-two million rows of data per risk run into the system. On average we complete three risk runs per day. Storing the data down at the lowest level of grain—the trade—means that we end up with sixty-six million rows per day. Storing it at the next level up—book level—then we end up with eighty-four thousand rows per day. The requirement from Ian states that the users need to keep the data for interrogation for eighteen months and archive it for statutory purposes for seven years. Calculating all this, we end up with a need for thirty-three terabytes for storing the data in big tables. If we reduce the grain to book level, then we end up with one hundred eight megs to store it per day."

Justin was realising that being data driven is a discipline for people building data systems as much as it was for making the business more efficient and effective. Knowing the size of the data enabled them to make sensible choices on the storage and the implementation of the system. It enabled them to make designs by scientifically understanding the limitations of the technology. "If we do want to store this data, at the current chargeback rates, we would burn through three and a half million pounds a year. Clearly, we are not going to be able to afford that, so we need to cut the data down."

The numbers on the size of the data really allowed the team to focus on the practicality of their approach. It brought to light that modern tools offer cheap storage; however, you still needed to be disciplined in how you use them. It was clear that capturing the right metadata was of huge benefit to the project. Jennifer looked around the room; it was clear that they had not done this calculation before. John was looking shocked.

"We need to cut down the amount of data we are storing. Can Ian go back to the business and push back on the requirements?" John asked.

"Before we do that, we need to look at the design and then play these numbers through with the new data model," Jennifer said.

Justin pulled up the next sheet. "On this next sheet I have drawn up the architecture that we are proposing where we join the data later in the pipeline." (See Figure 9.2.)

"I have taken the numbers from the calculations above, and I have applied them to the design and the structure of the framework that we put together in the last session." He continued, "By joining the reference data later in the pipeline at the reporting end and only using certain amounts of grain for some of the reports, then this is how the pipeline will work out." He brought up a new table showing that storing the data separately enabled them to reduce down the storage considerably. It also enabled them to optimise the reporting sets to only the data that the business process needed.

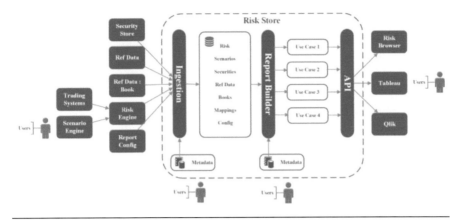

Figure 9.2   Justin's new architecture diagram taking into account the new design decisions.

"As you can see, the new numbers, although high, are achievable with the amount of storage that we have. I would think we would need to reduce the grain of the data stored daily beyond three months and then store grain for the month end. This gives us a total of five hundred gigs and fifty thousand pounds per year. This is going to be easier to ask for from the sponsors and management. Backing it up with the information in these sheets enables us to have meaningful conversations with them," Justin said.

"That makes sense; I will take this information with Ian to Brian and the steering committee. I think they will be able to compromise based on the data presented," Jennifer said.

"If we store the data separately, then that is going to mean that we need to join it back together to build the reporting data. We may have solved the storage issue, but all we have done is push the problem into a processing issue," John said.

He was right: by joining the data into big tables, the project had previously made a choice to sacrifice storage for performance. This was a typical balance that had to be made in the design of the system. Now, because they were proposing to undo that sacrifice, they needed to look at the processing and how they could achieve it with the technologies available. The fact that they could see the right compromise to make based on the instrumented data was a huge leap forward for them. They now needed to use the data again to establish the workload for completing the joins to generate the reporting sets.

The mapping sheets that they had in front of them laid out the data in a format that enabled them to understand the processing to produce the datasets required. They quickly adjusted the view of it to indicate the type of data and when the source was available. Applying the principle of joining data late, they were able to structure the sheets to see the flow that they would be building.

"The challenge that we have is that a lot of the joins to the base entities, like date, are joined multiple times onto the facts—for example, trade date, settlement date, value date, etc.," Ian observed.

"That is right Ian, the type of information that the users need changes based on the view or perspective they need to complete the analysis they are doing. If you are a trader, then you care about looking at the data from the perspective of the trade date. If you are within settlements, then you want to look at the data and the exceptions based on settlement date. If you are looking at post-trade analysis like risk and P&L, then you want to look at the data in terms of value date. Therefore, one dataset would never satisfy all the user's requirements. The joins must be made close to where the use case is realised to optimise that dataset for the user's individual purpose," Jennifer explained.

"The data that we are looking to combine is of all different types," John pointed out. "The risk data is time series, the organisation and the classifications are all hierarchies, and the reference data is all relational. There is not a single technology around that is suitable for storing all these types in the volumes that we need to process."

"That is true—it makes it hard to work through the technologies to understand which is the best for each. The advantage that we have now is that we know what we are trying to store, and it is logically arranged. Secondly, we know what the processing requirements are for the technology, so we can closely match them to pick the best option for the job. Thirdly, we know what is available to us based on the internal catalogue of technologies and what is available in the timeframes, so we can choose the best fit based on all these constraints and inputs and incorporate it into the design," Justin said.

"The way to do that is to take the use cases and the way that the users are going to work with the data and turn that into a set of patterns that the architecture will need to support," Jennifer explained.

"How do we do that?" Justin asked.

"Ian has been collating the datasets that the users need to complete their jobs. He has established the logical distribution of the data across the business. They divide up the world by asset class, with each product control group taking care of each asset class. This means that there is a clean distribution down the organisation hierarchy. Secondly, the workflow that they follow is that they verify the numbers at the aggregate level, comparing the levels and the changes to previous calculations. They use this view split by desk to identify anomalies in the numbers. When they find numbers that fall outside tolerances, they drill down into the data at trade level to pull out the affected books that have a problem. If I draw that on the board, then we have several paths that the users take that we need to support." Jennifer drew the pattern on the board (see Figure 9.3.).

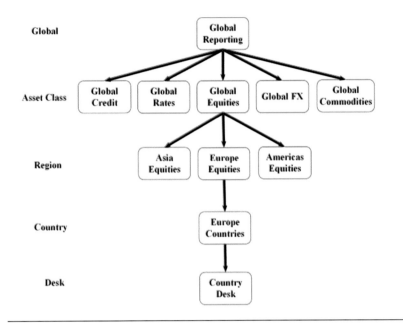

Figure 9.3   Jennifer's drawing of the organisation of the business.

"At the point of finding an anomaly, they resolve it or comment the difference and move on until they are happy with all of the numbers. Once they are happy, they submit their numbers to the head of the region, who is responsible for collating the data for the region and business. They pull out the most important movements and explanations for commentary to management of the global control functions, who are looking at the level of global numbers. When they have repeated this pattern for all the global businesses, the report is submitted for checking and final approval."

"What can we use from this information?" she continued. "We know that at each level they are interrogating the data via the book hierarchy and then analysing it by security and trade. We know to our advantage that not every user needs every level of grain in the system. The global users do not need trade level, and the regional users do not need trade level. Therefore, we should be able to come up with patterns that fit this querying profile. What is clear from the analysis is that not all the data or detail is required for all people at all points. What is also clear from this is that each business unit needs a different set of data and classifications to support their reporting and analytics." Jennifer pointed out the data from the requirements process—the data profiling and modeling which gave them this information.

"To build these individual datasets, we are going to need a process that sits over the raw data to pull them together efficiently. Given the nature of the data for risk, hierarchies, and reference data, we are likely to need to store them in different technologies," John reiterated. "If we are going to store them separately, how do we know that the data has referential integrity?" he asked.

"This is the key challenge in analytical systems," Dan said. "How do we know that the numbers that we are presenting are joined correctly, when the data has come from multiple sources? If they are not joined correctly, then the numbers cannot be trusted. In my experience there are two methods for achieving this: First, you maintain referential integrity throughout. This is a highly governed and organised environment, kept safe because they are not allowed to deviate at any point. This is a standard approach of online transactional processing (OLTP) systems. On the other end of the spectrum, there is data science, where data scientists pull many unrelated datasets together to join them to establish insights and blue-sky thinking. For the system we are building, we need to be between these two, where we can prove that the data we are presenting is accurate; however, we also want to enable people to innovate," he continued.

"It is all well and good saying that, but it does not answer the question," John said.

"Speaking practically," Dan explained, "at the time of the calculation of risk, the calculators had a set of data they used that represented the calculation, right or wrong. We need to pass this information through accurately and serve it up to the users. If we are collecting the data from the calculators, we need to make sure that we know which trade, security, market data, model parameters, and dates were used in the calculations.

"To achieve this, ideally, we need the primary keys of these datasets and the versions and dates. We can then collect the same information from the source systems, store it, and join it back up reliably. If we cannot do this, then we have got bigger problems. If the primary keys are reliable and accurate, then the data does not need to be attached and stay attached to the calculations. This will give us the flexibility to keep them separate and enable us to optimise the data pipeline. For the data that groups and organises the results, we can be more relaxed. It will need to have consistent primary keys but can be added and checked in the reporting layer. There are several steps we can take to ratify that the calculator's view of the data is the same as the reporting view:

- For completeness we can run checksums and joins across the primary keys.
- For accuracy we can intermittently run reconciliations across the reference data. That way we can ratify that the process is sound.
- Within the aggregation process we build in data quality checks.
- We can pick up early- and late-arriving facts caused by snapshot synchronisation issues within the join processes."

"What you're saying is that we don't force referential integrity through the pipeline, we allow data to travel separately, and when we join it back together, we make sure that it makes sense then?" John asked.

"Yes; essentially this is the bus architecture defined and explained by Kimball.[1] However, in modern architectures we need to be faster at joining data up in different ways to enable insights. That is the reason we follow the bus architecture principles but implement it differently," Dan said.

"If we are not joining data till later in the process, we are going to need a scalable engine that can accept risk and then join and reconcile it to the reference data," John said. "This type of capability comes from tools like Spark®. To work efficiently, we will need to make sure that the risk on disk is indexed correctly."

"If we look at the reporting sets that we require, then it should be clear what that index partitioning strategy needs to be," Dan said. "We should also be able to marry the query characteristics with the appropriate technologies."

"The process breaks down by business line and then territory, which is defined in the book hierarchy," Justin stated. "This means that the business will first select the subset of books that they have oversight on. This should then lead to a set of positions. When they have a set of positions, they will select the risk they want by filtering based on report. The query breaks down as follows," Justin grabs the marker pen and writes on the whiteboard (see Figure 9.4).

Figure 9.4   Justin's whiteboard diagram showing the sequence of the query broken down.

---

[1]   Kimball, R., Ross, M. (2013). *The Data Warehouse Toolkit: The Definitive Guide to Dimensional Modeling,* 3rd Edition. Wiley. ISBN: 9781118530801.

"For big territories, the risk is subdivided across risk managers by desk for the business line. For the analysis of the risk, the risk managers follow this pattern." He added the following diagram to the other side of the whiteboard (see Figure 9.5).

"Here are each of the steps in the chain:

- Check errors. Eliminate the errors in the risk that have happened upstream. Decide to continue or not.
- Check completeness. Reconcile the amount of risk records against the expected number of risk records from the active positions.
- Compare to previous benchmarks. This is where they establish DOD, MOM, and YOY calculations.
- Look at the outliers. Instinct and thresholds for change will determine if the risk looks right. For outliers beyond a certain threshold, they need to explain and potentially comment or fix.
- Drill into outliers. The risk manager will drill down the hierarchy to trade level to establish the cause of the large movements.

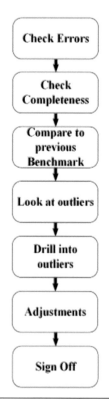

Figure 9.5   Justin's drawing of the sequence of events for analysis by the risk managers.

- Add adjustments. They will add adjustments to fix issues and commentary to explain larger movements.
- Sign off. They will sign off the risk."

"If we look at this and the work we have been doing, the query profile is clear," John said. "Firstly, aggregate across a subset of books. Run queries against previous risk dates to compare. Drill down a subset of the books based on the risk managers' responsibility to analyse. Run comparisons at this new level to check for differences to expectations," he concluded, looking pleased with himself.

"What is clear from this is that not everyone needs all of the data," Justin said. "The queries are split. When we go down to the lowest level of grain, it is only for a subset of the books. What is also useful for us is that the asset classes are split by the reports we need to produce. This means that the fields we select for one asset class can be different to the fields for another asset class."

"How does that help?" Harry asked.

"We can optimise the storage of the data for each asset class to remove redundant columns," Justin answered.

"One thing we need to be conscious of is that the next requirement is to aggregate by counterparts, so we need to make sure that the physical model will adapt to this in the future," Jennifer added this to make sure that the team were focusing on both optimisation and extensibility.

Jennifer was thinking ahead. Adding the counterpart would cause the lowest level of grain to explode. This would break the index optimisation that they had defined on book, because they would need to summarise by counterparty, and that meant it could come from any book. If they indexed completely by book for this solution, the system would have to do a full read of the raw data in storage if they then needed to read by counterparty. This would cause it to run slowly, and they might need to redesign the storage solution.

"Looking at the information presented here, there are different optimised solutions for each of the types of queries. Knowing what people are doing is a huge advantage up front, as it enables us to lay down the right patterns. I cannot see that there is a single layout that is going to meet all these different requirements. We are going to have to look at each use case in turn and then work out how best to solve it," she said.

"What we really need is a way to generate different datasets for the different analyses on the fly. We would then place the raw data into storage in a way that enables us to build the datasets rapidly for the different analyses," John summarised the solution design that Jennifer had drawn on the board at the meeting with Justin, back at the start of the process. He had made the journey from building queries directly on top of the risk store to having a layer that built targeted datasets for analysis quickly and efficiently.

John started to break down the problem based on the information that they had collated together. "At the region level, each analyst is likely to be querying a specific branch of the tree. This should enable us to partition the data effectively. They are first looking at summarised comparisons from today's number to the previous number. These feel like specific facts that we can build to cache the results. The comparisons are consistently the same comparisons, so we can look to build accumulating snapshots of the results, with the correct numbers added at the grain that provides the right comparison.

"After making this comparison, the analysts drill into anomalies. To support this, we can store the raw risk numbers for the drill down. At this stage they will have only a small subset of the books, so it will be much easier for us to make sure that the query is targeted and optimised for that use case." John was starting to confidently break the problem down. The data in front of him gave him the knowledge that he needed to make the right design choices and create the right datasets. What he was beginning to realise was that there would be many differently shaped analytical datasets that needed to be supported and that, as requirements changed, this set would change. Equally important to supporting the first requirements, he needed an engine like the ingestion engine to build these datasets rapidly and, equally, the ability to discard them when they were no longer needed.

He continued, "If the books are small enough, we should be able to handle this by reading all of the data onto the desktop and allowing them to analyse the data locally. This would reduce the number of queries that hit the big data store. We can use the front end to cache and provide this querying capability. If we can keep the users querying on the desktop, then we can make sure that the server is less busy. Looking at the split of the business, each set of users is only querying their specific asset group. Therefore, we can optimise the datasets on disk to be specific to the shape of the data for the asset class. This should enable us to remove the redundant columns that we currently store against each of the sets. This should reduce the complexity of the query processing to the state that we can reduce the impact on the data system. It should also mean that different parts of the cluster are responding to different queries from different users. This should help us to manage the resources," he concluded.

John was starting to see the irony of the situation. They were responsible for helping the users to use data to represent reality. To achieve that they had to embrace the data they had instrumented to enable them to provide data to the users. He could see how this information would help him to manage the workloads and the distribution of work within the system. He was in a flow state, solving all the challenges and thinking through all the requirements and how to solve them. The correct metadata had enabled him to see and focus on the solution. He would be able to size all the datasets and establish scientifically the scale of the system. He was becoming very excited about the prospects of solving the challenges in front of him.

"John, this is great work. Will you and the team be able to come up with a detailed design for the implementation?" Justin asked.

"Yes; there are some unknowns in the shape of the data and how it will perform," John replied.

"Is it possible to run some quick proof of concepts to be able to get some statistics on that?" Justin asked.

"Yes, we should be able to do that quite quickly; with the information presented here, we should be able to work out the exact performance metrics that will satisfy the system," John replied.

"We need to make sure that none of the reporting metadata is hard coded onto the risk data, so that the solution can support future use cases," Jennifer added.

"Yes, I understand," John replied. "We can solve that in the layer that builds the analytical datasets."

"How will you store the reporting metadata?" Jennifer asked.

"The data is different to the risk data. It is small, and it consists of relational and hierarchical data. It is probably best stored in our relational database, which will enable us to provide the users with the means to maintain it," John said.

"That sounds sensible," Justin replied. "Will you be able to query it effectively from there?"

"We will be able to build a post process that will combine the risk data and the reference data from the reporting sets," John continued.

"The data that we have here about the requirements and the underlying data sources enables us to know what it is that we need to build," John stated excitedly.

"We need to consider the fact that the users will want additions to the system. We need to build in the flexibility in the system to process additional data," Jennifer said.

"With the noise removed from the schema, then, as you mentioned, the core risk results are fairly consistently described by the data that generated them," John said. "We need to build the flexibility into the storage of the reporting metadata. This is where most of the churn happens now—here and in the attributes and classifications of the main entities," he continued.

"Do you know how to handle those?" Justin asked.

"Yes, some are just tables that have variable schemas. They can be managed easily with metadata-driven code. The more complex challenges are going to come from the addons to the reference data. These may pose a problem to the maintenance. In the short term we should be able to add extension tables called satellites in Data Vault® terminology to map new attributes onto the entities. The challenge comes in refactoring these so that it remains manageable," John said.

"That is how we handled the changes in the risk-reporting project," Dan said. "It proved effective in being able to respond to the additional needs of the users, but you are right, there does need to be a process where the new data is integrated into the main schema. We added additional sprints into the schedule with the knowledge of the users and sponsor to make these changes. Due to the responsiveness of the development team in delivering functionality regularly, they were happy to allow the extra time," he concluded.

"We need to make sure we model the schema to be able to hold the metadata that we have captured and will capture. Ideally, we want to make sure that the metadata is regularly updated to reflect the current state. That way it can be used for new projects and improved estimation of volumes, and it can also be used for capacity planning in the system. Once we have benchmarked the technology and established how it scales, we should be able to extrapolate the point at which it needs to be scaled up. This should help us to move to a proactive management of the system rather than reactive management," Jennifer said.

"That should be relatively straightforward. The metadata is consistent in its shape and size and therefore can be represented by some simple tables to store and maintain it," John said.

The team worked through the structure of the design of the system from front to back, establishing the shape of the data, the indexing, and the technology required to be able to query the information. The tools that they had were enough to handle all the workloads in the system; they just needed to utilise them differently. There was a lot of energy in the room; the technology leaders could see a clear path through to build a design that would deliver the use cases and be flexible enough to extend for future requirements.

Closing Questions

Design is about defining the problem accurately and then making the right compromises. Here are some questions to ask yourself:

- When you implement a data pipeline, do you have a design or do you rely on the iterations to get you there?
- If you do implement a design, is it based on technologies and fitting them to the requirement, or are you defining the requirement and finding the technologies to solve it?
- Do you know the characteristics of the technologies that you are using?
- Do you run into the situation where the technology is not able to solve the processing requirements in a suitable timeframe?
- Are you a workman who blames their tools, or a craftsman who builds elegant solutions?

Chapter 10

Iterations, Building Momentum

Key Concepts

The key to building data solutions is to deliver early and to build out. Often stakeholders will have less of an idea about the capabilities and the art of the possible than the data engineers and the data scientists do. Problems come in data systems from not managing expectations efficiently and effectively. Expectations are often out of line with what can be produced. The side effects of this are that the users either see the art of the possible and then raise the bar, or they are left waiting a long time for delivery, and then when it comes, they have moved on. Both can be terminal for the data project, both for the morale of the hardworking team producing the results and for the energy and the life of the project.

Having a constant feedback loop between the development team and the stakeholders and sharing the progress and the challenges builds collaboration and momentum in the delivery of the solution. This acts as a snowball, helping the teams to increase productivity, trust, and good communication. DataOps enables you to break down a project and to build iterations that help you to establish this momentum. Data projects by their nature will always try to get back to slow-release trains and waterfall processes; you need to know how to avoid this.

J ENNIFER RETURNED to her desk, feeling like not only were the team on the right track, but all of them were pulling in the same direction. With the positive energy she felt that they were ready to overcome all the obstacles and meet the deadline and the promises she had made to management. There was another hour before she was ready to head home. They were still under pressure, so she needed to collect her thoughts and catch up on emails and plan the next week. The first email was from Karen Lester.

"Hi, Jennifer,

"I need to catch up quite urgently. Have you got time next week to grab a coffee?

"Best regards,

"Karen"

Jennifer was grateful to Karen for providing James Cramer to the team. His work alongside Dan and Carl had provided all the information that had proved so useful in the design meetings. The data about data had really helped them change the team's outlook and direction. Hopefully, Karen was not getting cold feet, she thought to herself.

Jennifer quickly wrote a reply, offering Monday morning first thing. She sent the email and started working through the rest of her inbox. It was clear from the speed of reply that this was urgent. Karen sent through an invite for 8 AM Monday morning. Jennifer accepted the meeting and continued clearing her inbox. She next looked at the plan for the following week. She was confident now with the direction and speed of travel that the team had set. What she needed to do next week was to review the plans and effort to check that they were still tracking correctly.

She sent out an email to the team leads asking for them to update the planning and the tasks so that they could all review them early next week. It was getting late, and the week's efforts were starting to catch up on her. The team had turned around and were facing the right goal, but to achieve this had taken a lot of her effort. She was ready to recharge, so that she could spend her energy increasing the velocity of the sprints.

The light was starting to fade as she packed her laptop in the case along with the plans from her desk so that she could review them on the weekend. The building was deserted as she headed out of the door. As she was walking to the underground, she heard a familiar voice.

"Hi, Jennifer!"

She looked around to see Mark Denby, also heading home for the weekend.

"Hi, Mark," Jennifer replied.

"Heading home for the weekend?" Mark asked.

"Yes, it has been a busy week," Jennifer replied.

"I have heard. Some of the team are starting to really buzz with excitement. Justin mentioned at the water cooler that they could see a solution to the challenges of Aspen," Mark said.

"The team have really embraced the new effort and the changes that we walked through. It feels like we are making positive strides, but it is quite hard to tell from the inside. I am glad Justin feels that we are going in the right direction," Jennifer said.

"We are under huge pressure," Mark said ominously. "The regulator has looked at our previous submissions and has ramped up the rhetoric. They are threatening huge fines if we are not able to improve the information that we are sending them," Mark said. "Expect some news in the weekend papers about it. They have gone public saying that we do not have control of our data," Mark said.

"What was the problem?" Jennifer asked.

"The regulator has made comparisons of our risk information and our P&L information and concluded that they do not explain each other and are fundamentally different. They are partly right and partly wrong. The data we sent was from different dates and snapshots, and the P&L hierarchy is different to the risk hierarchy for obvious operational reasons; however, they have concluded that this is not acceptable and are talking about penalties. Senior management have asked for an explanation. They are starting to ask difficult questions with regards to what is going on," Mark said.

"That would explain why Karen was looking to grab a coffee on Monday morning," Jennifer said.

"Karen is under incredible pressure. The exec committee feel like they have spent millions on programmes around data and do not understand why it has not solved these problems," Mark said.

"The money was used as a tick box exercise to document the processes; very little of it was used to change the culture and the approach to embrace the governance," Jennifer said.

"They seem to think that spending money on the governance was the answer, and they're questioning where it has all gone and why they are having these issues," Mark said. "We are all under a lot of pressure."

Jennifer looked at Mark and could see the pressure on his face. She realised how important her programme was becoming. If it was not the case already, she would need to make sure that the project delivered the results to the deadline.

"Can you spare some time Monday to walk me through your plans?" Mark asked.

"Yes, of course," Jennifer replied, feeling that Mark did not really need to ask.

"I will set up a meeting for the morning," Mark replied.

"OK, I will clear my diary." It was apparent that Jennifer's weekend was going to be pulling together the plans and putting together a picture for Mark.

"I need to head to Bank tube station," Mark said. "Which way are you going?"

"I head home from Moorgate station," Jennifer replied.

"OK, I will see you Monday morning; have a good weekend," Mark said.

"And you," Jennifer replied. She was not sure that there would be much of a weekend, given the need to get the project out on time and the pressure that was now ramping up. It was going to be spent checking figures and looking for other areas of contingency that would enable them to hit the deadline with some time and effort to spare.

• • •

Monday morning came around quickly. Jennifer had pulled together the plans establishing lots of plan Bs over the weekend. The shape of the newly designed data pipeline gave her the ability to come up with lots of places where she could make compromises in the components that would not remove the integrity of the pipeline. It would enable them to get an end-to-end solution in place to hit the deadline and support the business processes with temporary or replaceable components in place. She believed that this would give them enough to provide a solution to Brian and team in a few weeks. Her thinking was that the last thing she needed was management panicking and jumping to the wrong conclusions and interfering in everything that they had started. She needed to meet Mark and Karen to gain support and then get together with her management team.

The morning air had a slight chill, and there was a strong breeze blowing through the buildings as she made her usual route through the city. The sun was just peeking above the buildings in certain parts of the walk and was enough to take the edge out of the temperature. The pavements were surprisingly empty given the time. She stopped off at her favorite coffee shop to collect a latte, fruit pot, and cereal pot.

On the way into the foyer, she walked through the barriers and into the building. She had an hour before she met with Karen, giving her time to look through her inbox and plan for the rest of the day.

Jennifer arrived at the coffee shop five minutes before the scheduled meeting. She waited inside the door for Karen. She saw everyone collecting their morning fix as they came into the office. Karen arrived just before time.

"Hi, Jennifer," Karen said.

"Hi, Karen," Jennifer replied.

"Do you mind if we get a coffee and head up to my office? We will be able to talk more candidly up there," Karen said.

"Sure, happy to do so, what can I get you?" Jennifer offered.

"Thank you, I will have a flat white," Karen replied.

Jennifer ordered the coffees, and they collected them from the end of the coffee bar and headed up to Karen's office. Her office was neat and tidy, with books all nicely lined up in the bookshelf, and her desk was empty and spotless, with just her monitors, keyboard, mouse, and mat positioned for her to work.

"I imagine you saw the press on the weekend?" Karen enquired.

"Yes, Mark warned me before I headed home," Jennifer replied.

"The regulators are really ramping up the rhetoric. They are unhappy with the progress that we have made. This comes from some analysis that they have done on our risk reports. The risk represented in the reports does not correlate with the P&L swings that are reported through a second submission," Karen explained. "They think that we do not have a handle on our businesses, and they are questioning our ability to manage the trading books. The differences are half related to the two different processes that we run to generate the reports, and half because the simple calculations that they have completed do not fully represent the risk that we manage. The problem that we have is that the explanations that we need to give are based on data that we produced six months ago, and we are not able to match the numbers that we sent them. The ops teams have been in all weekend piecing together old data, trying to come up with a representation of the numbers that we produced back then. The senior management team are really starting to lose their patience with the process. They believe that they spent millions on improving the data systems after the financial crisis, and they are unhappy that we are in this position," Karen explained.

Jennifer could feel the tension in Karen's voice as she was describing the issues. It was clear that there was a gap between the expectations of senior managers and what was going on in operations. She was clearly concerned that what they were planning would be able to fill the gap effectively.

"It is a challenge; temporality is always a problem in aggregation systems. The challenge is that the data used to produce the results after a certain amount of time needs to be deleted, because it is only there to explain the workings of the calculations and is not reported itself. Once it is deleted, you lose your link back to the source data. Most operational source systems are not written in a way to recreate history—it is too difficult given the number of changes that go on in them, so you are left with a gap," Jennifer described the challenges of keeping the intermediate calculations and datasets that make up the final submissions in a report.

"We should be storing the numbers in a way that we can explain them," Karen said.

"I know. The problem is that it is a lot of data and it needs to be configured from the start," Jennifer said. She was conscious at this stage not to provide ammunition for Karen to charge at Mark and the IT department. The last thing she needed in the period of building momentum was a lot of finger pointing and investigations. The truth was due to the way they were storing the results in big tables. The space they were taking up meant they had to prune lots of the data that was in the explanations to free up space for new calculations. The new model she had been working on with the team would address this by limiting the width of the tables and enabling them to store more metadata to provide context, but this would not be implemented in time for this crisis.

"I don't understand why it was not possible to keep the information. We have spent millions on this system. It should be able to describe what it did," Karen said.

"I think the problems are slightly wider than just the recreation of the results," Jennifer said, trying to steer the subject onto common challenges. "The finance department and the risk department use different categorisations of the book hierarchy to sum up the risk and P&L. This has always been the case and is likely to remain the case for lots of reasons, not least because they are using the data for different purposes. It is a constant challenge, because they work on different cycles for producing results, and they are producing results for different reasons. This means that the groupings will not reconcile to each other," Jennifer said.

"I know that, but the problem is those are the numbers the regulator is comparing, and they want to understand why they are different," Karen said.

"The challenge here is that due to storage and constraints the detail for these reports has been pruned, and therefore it is not possible to break it back down to explain the differences," Jennifer explained. She again was careful not to provide reasons for this, as it could cause issues if the finger pointing started. She knew that it was possible to resolve these issues once the new data model was deployed. It would be efficient enough to store the data that would be needed to explain the makeup of the numbers.

"Senior managers are starting to look at me and the budget that we have spent and wondering why this is not getting any better," Karen said.

Jennifer was now starting to feel the reason for Karen being so tense. The finger pointing from high was obviously starting to come down to Karen and put her position at risk.

"The work James Cramer is doing—he said that you are in the process of changing the models in Aspen. Why is this?" Karen asked.

Jennifer felt uncomfortable with the line of questioning here. She needed to answer in a way that would not incriminate the rest of the IT function. "The data models are changing to meet the functional and non-functional requirements. In the design sessions, we have collated the requirements of the users and found that they needed certain features in Aspen. I met with Brian Catts, who explained this. He also said that the next requirement for Aspen beyond the current implementation was to add in additional detail around counterparty. Having this additional information is allowing us to shape Aspen to take it into account. The second reason is that we needed to incorporate changes to the schema relating to the requirements that we discussed when we met previously. You want to have a system that makes it easier to produce answers to the regulatory questions. We need to make some changes to make this happen," Jennifer answered as diplomatically as she could. By tying the changes back to Karen's requirement, it would help deflect any potential witch hunt that might ensue.

"This whole thing is a complete mess. I do not understand how we are not able to build systems that work to provide the information that we need. We spend money with IT, and the job of describing the risk and P&L gets harder," Karen said.

"The issue here is not the fact that the money spent is not answering the challenges. The problem is that the exam question is getting harder. The regulators are getting more sophisticated in their analysis, and we have not got in front of the requirements. We are running to catch up," Jennifer said. "The only way that we can look to get on top of this is to improve the speed with which we can produce data and results and explanations. A lot of the work I am doing is to improve this velocity so that we can produce reliable results and datasets faster than the demand for them. This in itself is a double-edged sword, because the faster you produce the results the more demand comes; however, producing them in a reliable framework should give us the ability to achieve this without losing control," Jennifer explained.

"Do you know when you will have some results? I need something to show for the effort that we have put in," Karen asked.

Jennifer was annoyed at Karen's question. Most of the effort had been spent on documenting systems and not changing processes. Providing a CDO resource for a month was a drop in the ocean compared to the money already spent.

"I cannot do anything with the resource I have about regulatory submission that was made six months ago. What I can do is to make sure that these challenges are learnt from and applied to the future Aspen project," Jennifer said.

"Yes of course," Karen said, realising she had overstepped the mark. "I understand you have come to this only recently. I understand you are part of the solution and not the problem. I am under huge pressure, and I need to provide some answers,"

"I know. I will look and see if there is anything that I can do to provide you with some materials to explain how we are going to look to incorporate these new requirements into Aspen to make sure that the challenges go away in the future." Jennifer was careful to highlight that the work done now would take time to filter through.

"OK, thanks Jennifer, I would appreciate anything that you can give me," Karen said.

"No problem." Jennifer collected up her notepad and her coffee cup and headed out. That was difficult, she thought to herself. She needed to be careful not to raise expectations too high. That would be a sure-fire way to set the team up for failure, even if they achieved more than any other project had. She would have to collect her thoughts with Mark based on this meeting.

• • •

The meeting with Mark was in half an hour, just enough time to return to her desk and collect her thoughts whilst making a list of items to implement on the project. The pressure was ramping up, and Jennifer was starting to feel it. Despite this, she had complete faith in the plan and process they were following.

She headed into Mark's office. Tina had her head in the filing cabinet. She must have had a sixth sense, as she greeted Jennifer without interrupting her task.

"Hi, Jennifer," Mark said. "I imagine you saw the news over the weekend."

"It was hard to miss. Thank you for the heads up on Friday. It ramps up the pressure on the project," Jennifer replied.

"It does. We have been told in no uncertain terms that we need to get our regulatory submissions right," Mark said. "They are going to be especially vigilant on the Aspen submission. The senior management are meeting with Brian and myself to go through the detail on the project."

"That is going to make it harder to deliver and not easier," Jennifer raised. "How much extra reporting are we going to have to do?"

"Looking at it, I am planning to provide the aerial cover, so that you and the team can focus on meeting the deadline," Mark said. "I will need to meet with you more regularly to get the status information. My goal is to deflect everything back as best I can."

"I spent the weekend planning the project in a way that removes the delivery risk from the submission by getting a minimum viable release out into production as quickly as possible and then incrementally updating it to a more robust solution. The key is to remove the team from the critical path as soon as it is practical. With this plan, the production release will be delivered six weeks ahead of submission date, and the increments after that will come every two weeks. I am hoping that will allow people to focus on the numbers and the population of the reports rather than the IT." Jennifer showed Mark the plan that she had put together over the weekend.

"That sounds good, what are the compromises in the first release?" Mark asked.

Jennifer pulled out the deliverables sheet from the plan that listed the features for the iterations. "In the first release we will deliver the interface to the raw calculation numbers, the storage, and the formatted outputs with the ability to extract the data for the users to verify. We will then follow this up with the workflows and the analytics, which will enable the teams to run the investigations online. Finally, we will deliver the full end to end that connects in the regulatory formatted reports."

"If things go wrong, what is the contingency?" Mark asked.

"The contingency is that the business will have to manually do the regulatory submission," Jennifer said. "I haven't had time to present this to Brian yet, but from my previous experience, they are geared up to do this," Jennifer said.

"This could save us. When I spoke to the team in the previous submission, this was not possible; how are you able to bring this back earlier?" Mark asked.

"We have split the data pipeline up into separate parts, which will provide us with the ability to intercept the data at different stages and give consistent interfaces. We have instrumented the pipeline along its length rather than just at the end. It means we know the data quality at each point in the pipeline. We have separated out the data into core and reporting metadata. It means that we can quickly establish consistent datasets," Jennifer said.

Mark looked at the features and considered Jennifer's answer. There was a lot riding on her being right and being able to pull this off. He needed to quickly think through the risks and conclude if this was the right approach. The confidence that Jennifer showed describing the tasks and the confidence that Justin had described at the water cooler made him feel comfortable with the plan.

"OK, I will set up a meeting with Brian Catts to work through the contingency plan. Can you create a one pager for me based on this information that I can use to explain to the seniors?" Mark asked.

"Yes, I will add in some contingency to these timelines to make sure that we deliver and build confidence," Jennifer said, fully aware of the type of panic that occurs when things get tight and the amount of explaining it takes.

"I met with Karen earlier," Jennifer said.

"Yes?" Mark enquired.

"She is in a big panic about her role and the fact that the data does not tie together," Jennifer said.

"I am sure there is a lot of pressure coming down from above," Mark said.

"She is asking questions about why the work that we are doing now was not done six months ago," Jennifer added.

"OK, thanks for the information," Mark said.

"I think she is looking for a scapegoat around the fact that a lot of the CDO budget has been spent, and we are still no closer to having well-governed, consistent data," Jennifer said.

"A lot of the CDO budget got spent on documenting legacy systems in a static way. It became a free for all, spending money on governance systems and filling them up with metadata," Mark said.

"I know the only way to do that properly is to link the metadata into the change process and build incentives around its maintenance," Jennifer said. "Karen seems to be angling for material to deflect the focus."

"Don't worry, let me handle that. If you and the team can focus on these plans, then we should be able to hold off the tide," Mark said.

Jennifer left Mark's office impressed by his level of control in the most intense situation. She needed to meet with the team to bring them up to date with the news that they would have seen on the weekend. She knew that some of them would be concerned about the pressure that was coming down. They needed to focus and cut the delivery time to get them off the critical path. That would allow them the freedom to then start adding value in the increments and start to really help the business. Showing solidarity in that way would help to rebuild the trust in the group. Jennifer called the Aspen management team of Justin, Dan, Carl, and Ian to the meeting room at the side of the IT floor.

"Hi all, I just wanted to collect together to talk through the news that you saw on the weekend. The regulator is cranking up the pressure on Saturn, and the focus is on the Aspen deliverable. It looks like they are using this as a decision on whether we have our risk and P&L under control. This morning I met with Karen Lester, the CDO, and Mark Denby to discuss the implications. Mark spoke to me on Friday night and forewarned me that the news was coming. I therefore took the weekend to look at the plans that we have made to see how much contingency we can buy the business by removing ourselves from the critical path. The sooner we can do that, the easier it is for us to partner with the business in delivering the additional features that will make their job easier," Jennifer said.

"We have already crashed the plan," Justin said. "How do you propose that we make it shorter still?"

"You are right, we have already taken a lot out. The key to this is creating a minimum viable product that we can deliver that allows the users to produce the regulatory reports. This product will then be iterated to deliver more and more functionality." Jennifer brought up the delivery plan that she had drawn up on the weekend. "Based on the estimates provided, we can get iteration 1 of the solution out to the users in two weeks. We can then iterate the features through the remaining time. Iteration 1 is going to cause them a lot of manual effort, so it is key that we commit to delivering the additional features as quickly as possible afterwards. The way that we have organised the data should enable us to get this running efficiently and effectively," Jennifer showed them on the screen.

"There is quite a lot of rework to get the data models out in the new form," Justin pointed out. "There is a chance that we could make a number of mistakes."

"It is key that we deliver as reliable data as possible, or at least to provide information on how reliable it is," Jennifer said.

"We should be able to run the completeness and accuracy checks in the pipelines to provide this information to them. Some of the data quality (DQ) reports are part of the pipeline now. If we deliver them, we should be able to provide that information," Justin guessed.

"It is key that we highlight the DQ to the users. If we are going to help the business, it is important that we do not make their job more difficult," Jennifer replied.

"We should be able to convert some of our priority work into DQ reports that provide this information. We have built most of the queries against the sources. It should be relatively straightforward for us to build the reports against the pipeline," Carl said.

"That would be a great help. If you can do that, then we have a chance to add the DQ reports to the pipelines before they reach the users. John's team are going to be stretched based on this plan to hit the deadline. If you can take this off their workload, it will really help and enable us to make the data pipeline test driven. If we can build these tests into the iterations, then we should be able to speed up the release cycle." Jennifer liked the idea that Carl proposed.

"That makes sense, I can lend a hand with this," Dan said.

"We can provide checks on the reports and make sure they hit the user requirements," Ian said. "We know what the users are doing, so we are in a good place to check them off against their existing processes."

Jennifer was really impressed with how the team were rallying around the problem. She could see the path, and the team were taking responsibility for its delivery. She could confidently present the solution to Brian and the business that would meet the deadline with improved data accuracy from their sources of data.

"This is great, I will move the plan around for the next iteration based on what you have said. Can you go and communicate with your teams and make sure that they are happy with this?" Jennifer asked.

She adjusted the plan on her laptop and wrapped up the meeting, sending a copy of the plan to the team. She returned to her desk and checked her emails. There at the top was a meeting Mark had agreed with Brian Catts. It was scheduled in half an hour. She would have enough time to create a presentable form of the plan to talk through.

Jennifer headed over to Mark's office on the way down to Brian. He was just finishing up the meeting before and hung up his conference line. He gathered his notebook and headed out the door towards Jennifer. He quickly spoke to Tina, who was looking under pressure. She started moving his diary around and making notes.

They headed down to the ops floor via the stairs. Mark was fit and healthy, and he was often out running around the city at lunchtimes. Taking the stairs was a good way to work up some exercise minutes to compensate for the hours spent sitting down in meetings and behind a computer screen.

They arrived at Brian's office. He was talking to two of his team inside. He was much more animated than Jennifer had previously experienced. The team members were taking notes. He caught Jennifer and Mark out of the corner of his eye and beckoned them to take a seat at the meeting table. The energy and the tension in the air was palpable. Brian wrapped up the meeting, sent his team members on their way, and joined Mark and Jennifer at the meeting table.

"Hi, Brian," Mark said as Brian took his seat. "Thank you for taking the meeting."

"Thank you for coming down. You realise the amount of pressure we are now under. I have got every senior manager in the firm wanting answers on our plans to meet deadline. If it was not hard enough, it has just gone up a level," Brian said.

"Jennifer has put together a plan on how we can help you. We went through it this morning, and I think it takes a lot of risk out of the delivery of Aspen from the regulatory deadline," Mark continued.

Jennifer put the A3 sheet of paper onto the table that contained the plan.

"I looked at the work that we have been doing to reduce the dependencies and structure the delivery model. The simplified pipeline is due for delivery in the next sprint. This is where we have split the production of results and the reporting results," Jennifer pointed at the sprint plan and highlighted where in the schedule this was happening. "This gives you the data to check, and it gives you the first iteration of the reporting application. At this point we can use the next iteration to deliver a minimum viable product that you can use to manually run the regulatory submission. In doing this, I have taken Aspen from the critical path of the regulatory delivery. In the following sprint I have prioritised the development of the reporting front end to deliver the results along with a simple drill-down capability and the output for the regulator. To achieve this, I have lowered the priority of a lot of the workflow and the additional elements that will give you the complete system," Jennifer explained.

"Looking at the plan, the team can get a straight-through system from calculation to report in three weeks. That would give us another five weeks to the submission date. It should buy enough time to validate the submission," Brian said.

"We have already created an extract of the calculations so that you are able to iterate them quickly and get them right. This has led to there being a new risk run daily that your team is using to refine the calculation. They have been able to clean up a lot of the noise and really increased the velocity," Jennifer said.

"Yes, I know, they have been much happier since you have provided them with the data. If we have a delivery in three weeks, then what is the plan for the remainder of the time?" Brian asked.

"Firstly, we can run QA of the data and the reporting end to end. This should give us five weeks to make sure that the numbers are as they should be for submission. We then start to layer on the features that will complete the system. If we run out of time to deliver all the features, then at least the submission can be made," Jennifer explained.

"How come we have not been able to do this before?" Brian asked.

"The project ended up with dependencies in the wrong place. This was brought about by data being joined in the wrong part of the pipeline. By sorting out the flow to remove unnecessary dependencies, we were able to create deliverable sprints. Before this, the iterations needed the whole flow to be in place before they could produce results," Jennifer explained.

"The organisation of the data has been key to enabling this?" Brian asked.

"Yes, the problem with data is that it exists at different change velocities and for different purposes. It is not obvious what these are without a view of the business process. We collected the additional requirements to understand the business process, and we then established how it all worked. This has enabled us to simplify the underlying data models and break the dependencies," Jennifer explained. "We then profiled the data and established the optimised route through the pipeline."

"That makes sense; have you got information on what you can deliver to us, so that I can work through it with the team? They are currently scrambling to create manual processes to make the submission. With this we can probably cut down the work significantly and focus on the results," Brian said.

"Here is the high level of the deliverables for each sprint. I can send through the detail of what this means when I return to my desk," Jennifer replied.

"That would be great. I can then circulate this to the team, and then are you available to present the plan to them?" Brian asked.

"Yes, that is no problem. I will bring Ian with me, as he has been working with them to make this simplification," Jennifer said.

"Thank you, I will set up the meeting," Brian said. He was looking cautiously relieved at the prospect of receiving a helping hand from IT. Suddenly the mountain he and the team were looking at had just got considerably smaller.

Jennifer and Mark collected their things and headed out of the meeting room. Mark gave Jennifer a smile and said, "Well done. That has built a bridge between the two organisations. Now we need to maintain it. Can you set up a time in my diary three times a week to get together and talk through where we are? Tina should be able to free up some space. I should then be able to manage the messaging upwards to free up your time to make these deliveries," Mark said.

They walked back to Mark's office, where Tina was in conversation on the phone. Jennifer was about to make her job much harder and was not looking forward to giving her the message.

Jennifer spoke to Justin on the way back to her desk. She would need to be able to connect the development effort with the information she provided to Mark to make sure their path remained clear. The better the communication, in her experience, the less interference, and the energy of the team would remain focused on the task at hand. Providing her focus to the team would help steer them to the highest priorities and to get the solution out and off the critical path. The plan she had presented was already stretched, so she would have to remove blockers quickly without it impacting the timelines. The profile of the work should give them the attention of all the teams that provided dependencies to the project. She set about the rest of the day collating the information she would need to support the communication up the chain. The following day she would need to be on the ball at the standup to stay on top of the team and the momentum.

• • •

The standups were at 9:30 AM—enough time to allow the team to get in and to clear any outstanding support from the previous night. They split them into a data generation meeting led by John and a data reporting team led by Harry. Jennifer would then attend the combined standup among the team leads with Justin, Dan, Ian, Carl, John, and Harry.

They walked through each person who provided an update from the team. John started from the beginning of the pipeline.

"We have managed to get ahead on some of the pipeline tasks. We have the first iterations of the risk feed and Security Store. We have now decoupled this from the main flow to land its data separately, and we have done the same for reference data and book," John summarised.

"We plan to set up the tests on the feeds into the pipelines for testing their completeness over the next couple of days. This should give us the means to handle bad feeds effectively," he continued.

"We are blocked on the Rates Trading System (RTS). We can batch together old data into the risk engine, but it is not possible to get hold of the feed that will go into production. We are therefore flying blind," John added.

Jennifer picked up the issue. "That is not great. I will take it to Mark. Have we got a specification of the feed?"

"Yes, we sent it to them right at the beginning of the project. It just has not become critical for them," John said.

"Carl, can you and the team mock up a test feed based off the specification with test cases built in?" Jennifer asked.

"Yes, we can use the files we have got from previous projects and put something together quite effectively to cover the gap. We can then add some rows to represent the test cases."

"Right, we need to do that in the short term. It is good practice and useful anyway to help with continuous development and integration of the data pipelines. How long to get something up and running?" Jennifer asked.

"We should be able to put the sample files in place today, and we can then add in the test cases, which will take a little longer," Carl said.

"If we can get the test file in place today, that will clear the blocker, and I can then look to escalate this with Mark to get some progress on the main feed," Jennifer replied.

"Harry, how have you been going?" Justin asked.

"Yesterday we managed to complete the generation of the reports using the mocked-up data we were provided. It is not production quality, but the numbers going in are appearing in the reports in the right places in the outputs. We have completed all of the regulatory submissions so far," Harry replied.

"So, the business users can generate the outputs through the reporting. Will they be able to analyse the results?" Justin asked.

"We have produced the analytical sets to be able to generate the reports, but we have not configured any of the analytical use cases. There are degrees of readiness and sophistication, so I am confident the users will have the reports and the analytics soon," Harry continued.

"What is the plan for today?" Justin asked.

"We will continue to plumb in the analytics and the DQ dashboards. From now on that side of the project is incremental for us. We just need to prioritise the right outputs," Harry said.

"I can provide the priority," Ian said. "We collected this flag when we collated the new requirements."

"Great, can you make sure that you are synced up on this after the meeting? Ian, can you also schedule demonstrations with the users to collate feedback? It should lift their spirits and help to demonstrate that we are moving forwards together," Justin said. "Any blockers?"

"The main blocker that we have is connecting up with real data. Having the data sizes really helps in anticipating the scale of the solution. However, we need to test with some actual data and the true data size to give us time to optimise the user experience," Harry said.

"If we can get the mocked-up RTS file in the next day, then we can run our process through and get you some sample data in a couple of days," John said.

"That would help. That way we can make sure there is no heavy re-engineering left for us to do," Harry said.

"Anything else, Harry?" Justin asked.

"No, not from us," Harry replied.

"Carl, what have you been up to?" Justin asked.

"We have produced the test datasets for Harry, and we have been updating these. Harry has been able to test the solution as they have been building it. We will be spending the next few days creating test cases into the data to enable the teams to test exceptions. We are also building intermediate test cases for the data pipeline to help us spot issues early," Carl said.

"Any blockers?"

"No, nothing on our side."

"Ian, how have you been getting on?"

"We have been working with Harry's team testing the functionality so far against the requirement. The traceability matrix template is helping us work through this. We can link the use case to the deliverable and sign it off. The quality of what we are producing is really starting to improve. We are just coordinating the up-and-coming demonstration to the users. There is a lot of engagement, so we want to make it as good as possible."

"Any blockers?"

"No, nothing from our side. The key for us is to get as early sight of the new features as possible to enable us to make sure they are in line with the specification before demonstrating them to the users," Ian said.

"Thanks everyone for your time," Justin concluded.

Jennifer felt good about how the team was working to remove complexity and dependencies by decoupling the data and using it in the right ways. The team's morale and belief were really growing. The key for them was making sure that the momentum could be maintained. She needed to get an answer on the RTS file.

The RTS system was in Chris Way's area, so she would likely need to engage Mark to be able to unblock the issue. However, she decided to try the direct approach first. She got back to her desk and immediately picked up the phone to Chris to see if he was able to unblock the issue.

"Chris speaking."

"Hi, Chris, its Jennifer."

"Hi, Jennifer, how is it going?" he asked.

Jennifer sensed from his tone of voice that he was almost pleased with the heat that had fallen on Aspen. She took a breath and carried on.

"I have just come from the Aspen scrum, and we are waiting on delivery of the files from RTS. Would you be able to check and see when we can expect them?" Jennifer asked.

"Jennifer, I will go and check with the team. They have been incredibly busy building the latest version of the trading system. The business has prioritised it above anything else due to the benefits it will add to them. I am not sure where your file is, but I will check," Chris replied.

"Thank you, Chris. No doubt you understand how much scrutiny there is on the delivery of Aspen for the regulator. The project is key to Saturn to avoid huge embarrassment. Issues are escalating quickly. Please, can you come back to me this morning so that we can organise our plans effectively?"

"It sounds like you are having huge issues there—it is a tricky problem. We will come back as soon as possible; we like to be able to meet our deadlines," he said.

Jennifer could sense the power that this was giving him. He clearly wanted to prove that his way was right all along, and the new DataOps way was not going to embarrass him. She realised that the atmosphere between them was not likely to thaw quickly. She would need to make sure Mark was aware that RTS was critical path, just in case of any delays. Thankfully, Jennifer's regular meeting with Mark was later in the morning. She could provide him an update of the blockage without it sounding like an escalation. The last thing she needed was a confrontation that Chris would take pleasure from and would take her focus away from the great progress that they were making. She had walked in high-power environments for long enough to understand the posturing and the politics to be able to serenely float along and not get dragged into it. Key to her at this moment was maintaining the momentum the team had built up, knowing that it was much harder to restart it once it was lost.

Closing Questions

Building momentum is hard with data projects, but DataOps provides you with tools to help you achieve this. Here are some questions to ask yourself:

- Do you prototype the data or provide a sandbox area for users to demonstrate what they really want?
- Do your data and analytic projects have interim deliverables?
- Are you able to build demonstration sprints that show the art of the possible?
- Do you fail fast in a low-cost environment so you can share this and establish compromises?
- Is there an energy and confidence to your data engineers and scientists that they will meet or surpass expectations?

Chapter 11

Embedding Governance

Key Concepts

Documentation and governance are often the first things to suffer when pressure on the delivery team occurs. The longer that it is left to implement, then the harder it is to make it part of the structure of the code and the solution. If it is not done, then you will pay for this later down the line, when it must be bolted on and maintained separately. A well-designed data solution should be self-describing.

The benefits of this are that it will be transparent, a little bit like showing your workings out when you are answering an exam question. If the person marking your work can transparently see what you have done to get to the answer, then they can offer you marks for getting 90% of the right answer, but also understand the challenges of getting the right answer and offer you feedback on what needs to change. This is achieved in data systems by providing metadata alongside the results of the system. This metadata will take the form of data quality dashboards, lineage, and provenance alongside your results. In the finance industry, this practice is now part of the regulatory framework that is monitored by the regulators, and the executives in the sector are held directly accountable for the accuracy and completeness of their reporting and operational data.

ENNIFER HAD focused the teams—they had prioritised on the most important tasks, and she had started to clear the path for them. She was confident they were on the right track and progressing nicely. She had a chance to take stock of where they were and look at the next few phases. The key to the solution and delivering the embedded governance that she had promised Karen was tied up in the metadata that they had captured. They were now collecting the right data, which was important and had really enabled the team to understand the scope of the challenges and the design. The data had mostly been captured in spreadsheets, and this was not going to be a sustainable way to run things. She knew that the data pipeline and the instrumentation would be important to capture going forwards, both for general management of the platform and for finding and proactively managing faults and capacity before they were evident to the users. The data from the provenance would enable them to build future systems more confidently going forwards.

Jennifer knew that understanding the metadata terms and fields was required for the initial build, because how else could they build the right calculations and discuss the requirements effectively? The problem was that all the information captured was like a living document that needed to be maintained alongside the system and cared for like the code.

They needed to avoid the problems of the previous implementations:

- Where nobody really knew what data was in the datasets for the projects; this meant that every requirement was approached as a fresh problem.
- By not capturing the quantitative and qualitative information about the data, they did not have visibility of the challenges of future requirements.
- When the regulators were asking for data on the processes, it consisted of another fire drill to pull the data together and provide answers, quite often from reverse engineering the code.

These problems took the teams away from their primary responsibilities and meant they spent less time on value-add requirements. She would need to put down a technical feature to deliver a solution around metadata to address these problems.

She had mostly implemented the same solution on the risk-reporting project—this is where they had the means to turn most regulatory requirements around rapidly. She could pull the model across and plug it in. The key was to make the metadata drive the data pipeline and store information about its execution.

Alongside this, and by far the most challenging aspect, was capturing and linking the business meanings. The problem was that the generic words like risk, P&L, and position were great to describe the contents of the data, but they were very imprecise; yet storing the exact definition of every slice of numbers was too onerous. The challenge was that language was not precise enough to describe what a number was, and also that language tended to be local in scope. She had worked at other organisations in which their terminology was different for the exact same metric that Saturn called something else. Going between companies always took three months to acclimatise to the local language, acronyms, and terms. In the early days, you would always find yourself on the back foot, scrambling to understand and contribute on subjects you knew well because you were spending a lot of time in translation.

The challenge to Jennifer was clear. The business knew the numbers that they needed to present to the regulator and all the numbers that they produced during normal operations. Committees existed within the organisation to discuss oversight, reporting, and monitoring before any new type of instrument would be allowed to be traded.

The issue came in documenting the information in a way that it permeated through to the technical implementation and attached itself to the numbers that the IT systems produced. It was the same with Aspen: the BRD, although largely ignored by the implementation teams, contained all the formulas that needed to be called for the reporting, yet once the documents were written, there was no link to the IT systems. Therefore, this legacy way of working was not able to keep up with the complexity in the systems.

In the risk-reporting project, they had managed to change the generation logic to attach the specified metadata onto the data and then store it. They had created a metadata hub that would not only create the links, but in some of the components drive the ETL itself. The benefit of this was that whenever the logic changed, the documentation was also, by default, updated.

This gave several advantages: Firstly, it enabled them to report the information alongside the numbers in the form of lineage and data quality. Secondly, it enabled them to provide context-sensitive information directly to the user of the report. For the users who knew the information, this was a sensor check that they were reading the right data. For the more junior resources, it helped them to increase their knowledge of the data they were dealing with. The more senior resources would be able to spot the errors in the system from the definitions, or alternatively the errors in the definition, which was not uncommon. This community-type approach helped create trust and what Jennifer described as a democratisation of data. It had enabled her and the team an easy ride when it came to submitting answers to regulatory queries, and it avoided the archeology that sometimes came along with less organised systems.

The path of Aspen to date had not implemented these concepts prior to her involvement. The BRDs had not linked into the ETL processes and the formulas, and data had not been linked into the code. She needed to find a way to set them in the right direction. For the initial two-week sprints, this would not be possible due to the deadline; however, she needed a realistic plan to be able to provide a roadmap to compliance for Karen as well as implementing good practice for the team to avoid the need of future heroics.

She called out to Dan and Justin to create a consensus on the right items to add to the backlog.

Dan arrived first in Jennifer's office.

"Hi, Dan, take a seat. Let us wait for Justin. The purpose of this meeting is to establish the roadmap to move towards the centralised metadata store. We got most of the way there with risk reporting; however, we need to lay some of the foundations for Aspen. If we share with Justin what we did on risk reporting, we can work out between the three of us how to transition Aspen," Jennifer said.

Justin came in and took a seat.

"Hi, Justin, I was just saying to Dan that we need to look to implement embedded governance into the system to help us manage the data going forwards. We need to transition from heroics to proactive data management. When I say heroics, I mean burning the midnight oil in a reactive way when we are asked to explain why the numbers are what they are. Through looking at the callout log when I joined, a lot of the support calls that are made are to explain why a given number is the number that it is," Jennifer said.

"A lot of our time in dev tends to be the explanation of numbers. The teams that use our outputs tend to phone up with trivial issues. They have one number produced by the system and another number produced from a separate report, and they are not getting the same answer. Generally, it is down to the operator's comparing 'apples with pears.' They will have a number in a report that is filtered by a set of criteria compared against another number filtered by a completely different set of criteria. They are never going to match. If we could reduce the amount of these issues, then it would free up lots of time. Our previous attempts to do this have been to restrict the users to reports we have generated that are well explained," Justin said.

"What was the result of that?" Jennifer asked.

"The users used the system less. We ended up with fewer support calls, but they were doing a lot of their work outside of the official systems. They only used our reports as a check against the manual processes that they had created," Justin said.

"On risk reporting, we took a different approach," Jennifer said. "We provided metadata alongside the real numbers so that we were able to make it clear what had been generated. In the later versions of the system, we displayed the same metadata that was being used to generate the reports. That way we could give them self-service data, but with the added benefit of having well-described outputs. It meant they were less likely to ask us what they had done, because all of the data was directly in front of them," Jennifer said.

"That is a long way from where we are now," Justin said.

"I know, but what I want to start to do is to describe the direction that we are heading and the steps that we will be taking. After we hit this immediate deadline, I want to make sure we have a roadmap that I can present to the management to help us move to where we need to go. Otherwise, we will probably get pushed towards the next most important requirement without the means to get our own ship in order," Jennifer said.

"Is that something that we can break down?" she asked.

"I cannot do that technically, as we will need input from the team. I should be able to do it functionally. Presently, John and Harry are flat out, and they are making good progress towards the deadline," Justin said.

"That makes sense. If I have a functional description of what we are trying to do, then we can use that to be able to provide the vision of the solution to the stakeholders as early as possible. This should enable us to ask for the time to remove some of the technical debt that this solution will no doubt create," Jennifer said.

"The vision for the system is that the metadata used to capture requirements is what gets implemented in the system and is maintained by the system change process so that it stays in line with the implementation. This should ideally be the metadata driving the transformation process," Justin started with the mission statement. "The reporting of the processes can then be driven by reporting on the metadata."

"To achieve this, we need to build a repository to store the metadata captured from the requirements process and the instrumentation of the pipeline. The refinement of this needs to be available to the people who know about the data," Justin continued. He drew a metadata box on the whiteboard, with inputs from the system. He then drew up the ingestion engine and the storage, post processing, and reporting flow on the white board, with the consumers of the reports and the workflow on the end. He connected the glossary function to the metadata store and then added a glossary user interface alongside a lineage user interface serving up the information to the users, but with a two-way arrow for them to be maintaining the metadata as well as reading the metadata. He added a metadata reporting function onto the diagram with the outputs and added a CDO consumer. He then started to list down the types of metadata that he saw in the system. Once the diagram was complete to the best of his knowledge, he started adding colour for the components that they had, the components that did not exist, and the components that would need to be changed to incorporate the vision. After around ten minutes they had a diagram that provided the information that they needed (see Figure 11.1).

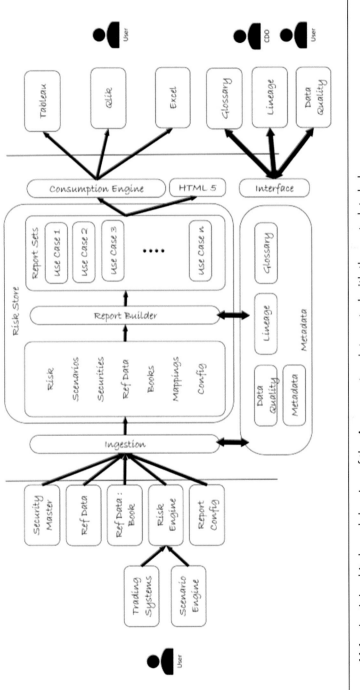

Figure 11.1   Justin's whiteboard drawing of the Aspen system integrated with the metadata hub.

"This is great," Jennifer said. "Can we sit down and list the items on the diagram that we are going to need to build and change as features and enablers? We can then make sure they are on the backlog. For some of these features, there are components in the risk reporting library that could enable us to accelerate the effort. For instance, they have implemented a metadata ETL system, and they have the starting of the metadata hub. This is not as comprehensive as it needs to be, but it potentially can be lifted out. The architecture that we built was scalable both horizontally and vertically using a component and service-based architecture," Jennifer said.

"We also have the data model for the metadata store that should be consistent with what we need here," Dan added.

"We need a way to capture the requirements that is consistent with the way it is used or instrumented from the pipeline," Justin continued. This needs to be stored in the metadata hub. The hub will need to be built to capture all the types of metadata; we have the risk-reporting solution as the first implementation of this store. We need a metadata-driven pipeline that enables us to start to turn the solution from the code to metadata. We need to attach a user interface to the metadata hub to enable the users to observe the flow, understand the flow, and interact with the documentation around the flow. The hub should serve up definitions of terms and fields to the reports and the analytics to improve the trust that the users have. This will help enable us to democratise the definitions and improve the knowledge.

"As an extension to the metadata hub," he continued. "We will capture sizing, volatility, and other statistics about the data to help us to build knowledge for future extensions. It will also enable us to manage capacity and change management activities professionally. We will use the hub to capture data quality information—that will enable us to deliver this alongside the results to make sure that the users of the data are able to understand the quality of the insight.

"Finally, we will create the means of self-service through enabling the data pipeline to be driven by the metadata and, to some extent, driven by the users themselves. We will need to break down these items into further detail, but I can establish the gap and the work required to achieve this," Justin concluded.

Jennifer sat back and looked at the list; the structure and the items were perfect for the implementation of the future vision. More importantly, it would enable them to keep up with demand. The IT team could focus on the components and the infrastructure, and the users would be empowered to answer their own questions. The self-documentation would serve a couple of purposes. Firstly, it would limit the needless investigations required every time the users used the application incorrectly, and secondly, it put the ownership of the system back where it belonged—with the users who understood the data and could feel empowered with using it.

She now needed to create a presentation that she could use to make sure that the vision would be realised and the project would be allowed to do the necessary work to make it happen. The teams were completely focused and pursuing the goal in front of them. Jennifer knew that when they hit the deadline, there would be a huge surge of attention and an underlying belief in this way of working and that it should be repeated. She knew that they had built up technical debt that they needed to unwind. Not only would her presentation need to be compelling, but she would also need to time the conversation carefully. Presenting the future before the crisis was over would come across as arrogant. Presenting it too late, and people would have their focus on the next crisis.

She spent the next few days staying on top of the team and iterating the presentation. The management summary was the key page, but the rest would need to stand up to scrutiny. She had most of the material from the sessions with the team, and she spent time iterating back and forth with Justin and Dan to refine it. The delivery of the latest sprint was coming up. In this they would be rolling out the means for the business teams to answer the reporting needs for the regulator. It would give them everything that they needed to hit the deadline and lower the pressure on the IT team. She was going to wait till this was rolled out and with the business to then make the presentation to the stakeholders.

• • •

The Monday demo for the first release was coming around quickly. The team had all volunteered to give up parts of their weekend to make sure that it went in smoothly. Jennifer arrived in the office first thing to monitor the run book for the release. The release was to be run by the support team, coordinating with the infrastructure team and the development team. This was typical for the bank to provide the controls necessary around the production environment. Due to the configuration of the data in the system and the disks, the release was scheduled to take a couple of hours. Jennifer busied herself working on some additional features to her presentation.

After a couple of hours, the release was complete and handed over to the development team to run smoke tests to verify that it was released correctly and the components were configured correctly. Once complete, then the team ran through full end-to-end tests, and everything seemed to be working as expected. The calculation team launched a first run of the data, and the data analysts added all the patches required as data files to be able to produce results. They ran through a test iteration, and all was well. Ian drove the user interface and tested the accuracy of the reports and the features in the release. Due to this being the first iteration, not everything was included, but it was important that some of the features would be included to enable them to build the trust with the users.

After verifying that the system was working as it had done in the test environment, Ian set up a meeting with the users to demonstrate the end-to-end functionality for Monday morning. Before leaving on Saturday evening, the team kicked off a calculation run.

On Sunday John logged in and kicked off Aspen manually. He then logged in every hour or so to watch the run through. Jennifer was monitoring the status from her mobile phone. The comments from John's status reports were getting more and more animated. The optimisation of the flow of data through the system and the speed of the storage was absolutely flying. What had taken hours before was now taking minutes. The concern about whether things would finish or not was gone. Not only would it finish in a few hours, this would leave them with the chance to rerun the process up to four times before it would be needed on Monday.

At 12 noon on Sunday, John sent out an update. "We have a problem."

Jennifer quickly got onto the dedicated conference line with the rest of the team.

"Hi, John. What seems to be the issue?" Jennifer asked.

"The process stopped whilst it was trying to create the risk aggregates," John replied.

"What was the error message?" Justin asked.

"It says that there are no sector groupings for the security classifications. It says too many results have failed and therefore it was stopping," John replied.

"Can you provide me with the sector groupings file?" Carl asked.

"Sure," John logged onto the system and picked up the sector groupings file and sent it through to Carl. Carl quickly looked at it on his computer. There were only a few hundred groupings in the file.

"They all seem to be here. This is the file that we have been using in the user acceptance test environment. It does not look like it is down to the file," Carl said.

"John, can you have a look at the configuration and see which files it is picking up?" Justin asked.

John went to the configuration and found where it was looking for the sector mappings. "This looks OK," he said. "Wait a minute, this has got the wrong path. It is pointing at the configuration that we run in test and not where the files live on production."

"Can we get that fixed?" Jennifer asked.

"Yes, I will contact support and get them to patch it. It must be something in our release process between test and production. I will make a note to fix this in the deployment scripts. I should be able to insert the new file and then restart the process. It should then build again incrementally from where it got to," John said.

Jennifer sighed in relief. The last thing they needed was to have a failed release. It was good that the configurations and the controlled data pipelines meant that the processes were reentrant. It was also great that they stopped when they found issues.

They ended the call, and John went about making the patch to the release and kicked it all off again. The process got another ten minutes in, and then stopped again. This time John quickly looked at the issue and realised that the same issue existed in the country groupings file. He quickly fixed it again and sanity checked all the other configurations for the same issue and kicked it off again. Two hours later it had all completed within tolerances, and the results were ready to look at.

The team got back onto the conference call. "What is the next step on the run book?" Jennifer asked.

"Automated tests," Justin replied.

They kicked off the automated tests. These verified that, as a minimum, the numbers that had entered the system were appearing in the reports correctly. It was fundamental that the pipeline was intact and the data was complete.

It was down to Ian and Carl's teams to go through the outputs and sanity check the reports and the output. After a few hours of checks and balances, they were confident that the reports were looking as good as they could and that the system was ready for demonstration.

Everyone for one last time got onto the conference call. Jennifer went around all the team to check that they were OK to sign off on the release. Each in turn approved, and the release was signed off. It had been a long weekend, but it was worth it. The new data pipelines had been released in the first incarnation, and they had performed admirably. They had several things to fix, but the release processes would only get better and better from here as they refined the automation and improved the run books. Everyone signed off and left the call to enjoy their Sunday evening.

• • •

Monday came around a little too quickly. The whole team, to their credit, all arrived bright and early. The demonstration of the system was due at 10 AM.

Ian was ready for the demonstration, wanting to show the users where they were. He had prepared a script to go through the functionality and to demonstrate the new features and reports to the users. The demonstrations were every two weeks at the end of the sprints. The continuous delivered code and release enabled them to build a demonstration rapidly.

Harry and his team had already been demoing the reporting front end and iterating it to a solution, but this would be the first time that it contained the calculated data. The sessions were booked in for thirty minutes and involved the business users and the development teams. Ian coordinated and was the key demonstrator. The attendees arrived promptly for the call and were keen to engage. Most of the key stakeholders attended, and they had some delegates representing different parts of the upstream pipeline.

Ian started off by firing up the user-reporting interface. It would show how the users could access the system. They had set up the release mechanism for this iteration with the ability to connect to the production system. The system popped up and immediately shared the status and a level of data quality of the most recent risk run. The checks along the pipeline fed the data straight into the front end. Most of the checks were 100% because of the hand-holding the team had done over the weekend. In normal circumstances these would be lower, and the team would use the output to build up rules to improve the overall flow. Ian demonstrated that clicking through the data quality indicators gave the teams plenty of description of the issues that had occurred. In this case a few of the securities had not mapped onto the risk, causing some of the classifications to be missing. The patch on the missing RTS feed was OK but was not perfect.

Ian went on to the rest of the functionality in the front end, showing the reports that had been completed and the status. Clicking on a report took the user through to the report itself, demonstrating the format of the data and the output. He walked through the reports one by one, showing the users the ability to see the results, but also to get hold of the raw data. This was a compromise they needed to make at this stage until they had the chance to complete the validation screens. They were due in subsequent iterations. Given the data literacy of the users, they would be able to analyse the raw outputs.

Jennifer was observing the whole demonstration on her computer. As each feature was demonstrated, the tension started to be released. All the features on the release schedule were being demonstrated step by step. They had made slightly more progress than expected, but the features that were added on top of the sprint would be held back to the following demo.

At one point in the demonstration, the key operations user could not help themselves and said, "This is the best thing we have seen from IT in years." Jennifer was totally shocked. How could they have not seen something like this before? The team had only put together part of the solution at this stage.

Ian got to the end of the demonstration and then showed the users where they could access the system for themselves. He gave them the email address and phone numbers to log feedback and then opened the floor to questions.

Most of the users confirmed that this was great and a massive step forward. There were a couple of questions around the schedule of the next releases. Ian confirmed and listed the features and the capabilities that would be included, and the demo naturally ended.

Jennifer wanted to use the positivity of the session with the team. She quickly called a post-demonstration scrum and retrospective. All the team leaders turned up to the meeting room on the side of IT. The energy and the bounce in their steps were clear to see. John, who previously had a look of a man going through the motions, had a big grin on his face. They had managed to get an early iteration out to the users with all the expected features and no excuses. Not only that, but they had also removed themselves from the critical path.

Justin was equally pleased. He quickly seized the moment. "All, that was a great demo and release. We have not only met expectations, but for the first time in a long period we have exceeded them. There was huge positive feedback from all involved from the business. Well done everyone for getting us to this point. We are now at the stage where there is enough of a system for the business to make the next submission.

"We have a lot of ways that we can move the system on and make the submission process smoother. With what we have delivered, there is still a lot of work that the users need to do to get to the point of sign off. We have a list of features that will enable us to really help them cut down that work, to make their lives easier. Later this afternoon we need to put together the next sprint plan."

"Well done all, that was an amazing team effort. We have been dynamic, efficient, and effective by doing the right things well," Jennifer added. "As Justin says, we have a real chance of helping out the end users to achieve a smoother, more pain-free journey and build a lasting relationship."

"We need to focus on supporting the current release and making sure that the users are comfortable using it. We need to clean up any hangovers and fixes in the source control that we applied to get the release to work. This afternoon I will schedule the official retrospective and the planning for the next sprint." Jennifer wanted to maintain the discipline that had served them well in this sprint. The team all got up and moved out with big grins on their faces.

Jennifer went to her office and sat down with a sigh of relief. Being off the critical path was a huge weight off her mind. She now felt a sense of responsibility to the business to assist them with the delivery of the regulatory submission and to automate many of the checks and sign-off processes, as well as providing Karen with the implementation of DataOps governance.

She had not been sitting down long when the phone rang. "Hi, Jennifer speaking."

"Hi, Jennifer, it's Brian."

"Hi, Brian, how are you?" Jennifer asked.

"I am good, thank you. The team have just got back from the demo, and they are really buzzing. They said the system is delivering all of the reports they need for the delivery of the reg submission," Brian said.

"Yes, that is true. The plan we went through before this sprint has been delivered, and they have access to the first iteration," Jennifer said.

"That is great, we have what we need to meet the next submission," Brian said.

"That is true, although there is a lot we can do to make the process smoother from the delivery of the reports through the analysis, commentary, and sign-off process. We are fully focused on these elements from this point on. We wanted to first make sure it would be possible to deliver the output and then to start adding value," Jennifer added.

"Where you have got us to in a short stretch of time is a huge step forward. Thank you," Brian said.

This was Jennifer's chance to now put forward the presentation that the team had spent time on.

"No problem, Brian. I would like to walk you through the plans and the vision for the system. This is additional detail on our first meeting and vision phase. It is important to realise that what we have delivered is only starting to put shape on what we should be delivering for you. Can I put some time in the diary to walk through what we need to do to make the types of delivery we have achieved this week a regular occurrence?" Jennifer asked.

"Sure, my diary is free on Thursday. Do you want to send me an invite?" Brian replied.

"Yes, I will send one through straight after the meeting," Jennifer said.

"Thanks, Jennifer," Brian said.

"No problem, Brian, see you then," Jennifer said.

That had gone much better than Jennifer had imagined. She now had a slot where she could make sure that they were not left with the technical debt that they had knowingly accrued. She now needed to have the same conversation with Mark to enable the vision to be realised.

Her regular meeting with Mark was coming up later that morning, and this would be a good opportunity to put the plans forward and to get consensus for the plan.

• • •

The meeting with Mark came up quickly. She headed across the IT floor to his office and stopped outside to check with Tina. "Hi Tina, is Mark available?" Jennifer asked.

"I think he is just finishing a call and will be available shortly," Tina replied.

Mark acknowledged Jennifer through the glass office wall. He had the phone still against his ear. A couple of minutes went past, and Mark waved Jennifer in.

"Hi, Jennifer, take a seat, I will be over in two seconds," Mark said.

"Hi, Mark," Jennifer said.

Jennifer took her usual seat in the corner of the office looking out. Mark finished typing and grabbed his notebook.

"I spoke to Brian this morning. He said that what they have will enable them to hit the deadline. He was really pleased," Mark said.

"As we discussed, the key was to get the minimum viable product out there to remove ourselves from the critical path and remove the risk to Saturn," Jennifer replied.

"That is great and gives me lots of opportunity to hold off the tough questions from above. So, what next?" Mark asked.

"As you know, we have delivered only part of the overall use case; we need to implement all of the functionality. By responding to the challenge in the way that we have, we have created some technical debt that we need to unwind. If we do not, then the project will go in the same direction as in the past and not provide the flexible environment and solution described in the vision," Jennifer said.

"What do we have to do to eliminate this technical debt?" Mark asked.

Jennifer handed over the presentation. "I prepared this presentation last week with the team. I did not want to present it until there was the right level of trust in the plans." She turned to the management summary page at the front. "The vision for the system is the ability to empower the users with information not only about the business, but about the data they are using in the form of data quality, terms, and business meanings to enable the users to work with the data system largely independent of ourselves. This will free up more of our time to incorporate more data and to build more features and capabilities.

"Each request for information either about the underlying pipeline or the numbers is taking up an average of one week of a developer's time to resolve. Some are very small in terms of checking errors or outliers. Other requests around the regulatory explanations take weeks or even months. My goal is to reduce this down to next to no time at all. This should free up the development team to be more productive and to deliver additional features to the business. Done correctly, we can have the business users servicing their own requests," Jennifer explained.

"That makes a lot of sense," Mark said.

"Thank you, the challenge is not describing and implementing this, it is managing expectations whilst we are implementing it. There is always a push to keep doing tactical work, much like this last iteration, that will mean that we build up more and more technical debt until the point that we are no longer able to function due to the need to manually hold the system together," Jennifer said.

"What you are asking, to paraphrase, is for my support to enable you to implement this plan so that we can get to the vision," Mark echoed back.

"Yes, there will be a natural pressure to move to the next critical situation. I need support in making sure that we are doing what is important and non-urgent," Jennifer said.

"OK, the support is there. What I need is a discipline that the effort is quantified and measured. We need to deliver the things the business needs alongside the capabilities to deliver them. Too many projects have disappeared into framework land and never come out. It is important to make sure that there is a balance," Mark said.

"We are implementing an agile solution with input from the users. The only change that we are making is to ensure that the technical features do not get overridden by the business priorities every time. The key for me and the process is that we have established trust with the business users. This should enable us to share the responsibility for the system and to make the right choices. I therefore do not expect to need to argue too strongly for doing the right thing, but when I do it will be for a good reason."

"OK, it makes sense. What do you need from me?" Mark asked.

"Firstly, please can you review the plan I have created and let me know any feedback. I am scheduled to present it to Brian in a couple of days. Secondly, approval to present it to Brian and the steering committee," Jennifer asked.

"OK, I will review it today and come back by the end of the day," Mark said. "Anything else?"

"No, nothing from me," Jennifer said.

"Make sure you congratulate the team from me. We are not out of the water yet, but they have really made a huge difference," Mark said.

"Sure, thanks Mark." Jennifer left the meeting pleased to be given the remit verbally to move forwards. She would wait for approval and then present the vision to Brian.

• • •

The next couple of days passed quickly. The team moved quickly onto the tasks for the next delivery. There was minimal support required on the release. Most of the instrumentation was catching errors and stopping the pipeline when they reached a pre-defined threshold. Mostly this was down to timing issues between the reference data and the main risk payload. It served as a reminder for the users to update mappings and to insert supporting data. The new level of information about the processes that they had at their fingertips meant that they could do their work with minimal need for IT support. This was allowing the development teams to work rapidly through the features in the system.

Mark read the proposal that Jennifer had produced and was fully supportive. Things were turning around. For Mark, the gamble to bring Jennifer in to run the project was paying off. His rivals were starting to back down. Word had reached senior management, and they were being more supportive. He wanted to show his full support for the effort and planned to attend the meeting with Brian. With the sponsor and IT management backing the plans, they would be able to provide Jennifer and team the aerial cover to deliver the right solution.

They turned up together on the operations floor at Brian's office. He was busy with his team leads deep in a meeting. As soon as he saw them waiting outside, he waved them in.

"Hi, Jennifer and Mark, please meet Sophie Lawrence, Joseph Link, and Julian Barnes. They lead the regulatory submission teams. They have seen what has been achieved in the Aspen delivery, and they want to have input on the future vision," Brian said.

Jennifer thought to herself that this was a huge turnaround. Up until this point, Brian had wanted to run the meetings himself, and now his phrase "they want to have input" was very different to "I told them to have input." This was exactly what was needed. The IT team needed to get good feedback and be part of the business team to enable them to deliver on the real requirements. This did not come from well-constructed business requirements documents. This came from understanding the business processes firsthand and then being able to help the business deliver on their objectives.

The group all introduced themselves and their responsibilities. Mark and Jennifer explained their roles and proceeded to walk through the deck that Jennifer had produced. The team leads were asking questions and interacting in a way that they had not done before. They made suggestions on how to improve the data flows and the processes to optimise their work.

At the end of the meeting, Jennifer got the impression this was now a shared plan. It was something that Brian and his team had bought into and had genuine belief in being delivered.

Jennifer had come to the meeting with a best-case scenario of getting approval, but she felt that she had ended up getting a lot more. Mark sat quietly, letting the meeting go ahead, observing the interaction and providing the support to allow Jennifer to proceed. At the end of the meeting, Jennifer had written a page of notes on what needed to change and be actioned. The meeting ended, and Brian took the opportunity to thank Jennifer for getting them to where they were. "The difference in the engagement approach has made it possible for them as a business team to believe that they would hit the deadline. The big thing for me and the team is that we now believe that we can deliver on our business goals through IT and not despite IT."

Mark and Jennifer got up and left the meeting. Jennifer felt mightily relieved that all the plans had been signed off and refined without the need for a lot of convincing. They walked back up the stairs and back to the IT floor.

Closing Questions

Embedding governance in a solution is key to minimising the amount of effort that is needed to provide it when it is required. Here are some questions to ask yourself:

- Is your data presented to the consumers with transparency?
- Do you build governance into the pipeline as part of the development process?
- Are you aware that governance is an important part of the delivered solution?
- How long does it take you to explain the numbers in your analytical solutions?
- Are the users able to correct the quality of the data within the system, or do they do it post system?

Chapter 12

DataOps Realised

Key Concepts

DataOps enables you to put the right work in the right hands and to enable teams to collaborate effectively on the business goal and vision. This teamwork really transforms the velocity with which a solution can be built. In many projects, by building this collaboration, we have been able to increase productivity towards a solution by multiples greater than two to three. Another advantage is that the solution is more likely to be suitable with what the users need and delivered when they need it.

The challenge with data systems is that the users are the SMEs of the data, and the technology team's role is as facilitators for the users to work with and leverage the data. Often this relationship gets skewed due to several reasons—for example, users are too busy to carry out this role, IT assumes that it can do it, and the consequence is that the wrong people become responsible for the wrong roles.

DataOps is about establishing the collaboration to solve problems, where each stakeholder can play their role, and the feedback from this is realised early and often to create reassurance that this is a better way to work. The result is reduced drama around the solution. In one example, a stakeholder on a project that we worked on said, on a demonstration call six weeks into a project, "This is the best thing we have had in two years." These are the types of experiences that everyone should be having with their data projects.

THE NEXT few sprints progressed, with the team efficiently working through the backlogs and features that had been scheduled. Gradually, more and more functionality, analytics, and governance rolled out the release train and integrated into the platform, making the business users' lives more and more simple. The amount that the pipeline could be changed through configuration and metadata increased, making it simply training or data analyst work to respond to the changes in the reports and analytics. Even some of the mappings and flows were being amended by the business users under Ian's guidance. The pipeline was flowing through in a few hours, and the speed of the flow could be changed by allocating more machines. This was enabling support to respond to bad data and still push the batch through in time.

• • •

The submission date came, and the users had worked through and run all their checks and balances efficiently. The numbers were as right as they could make them, and where they were adjusted, commentary was tagged to the report to explain the purpose for the correction. The true test of the system came when senior management ordered an audit of the results and the evidence. This was going to be a lengthy procedure, where they wanted in-depth verification of the submission to validate the numbers, the sources, and the calculation.

A team was set up specifically for the purpose. They started to ask for extracts of the data and the traceability information and started collecting golden source information and running checks. Under the old methodology, this would have been a cause of huge anxiety for the business and IT, where they had no intermediate data. In the new system, the instrumentation they had had already output completeness calculations and accuracy reports. The comparisons to source data were already available in data-quality dashboards. The users had run their own checks and balances back to their own copy of the truth and had confidence that it was real. In the process, they spotted several shortcomings in their own tools and reports and had to correct them to continue to run them.

The audit team continued to question numbers and formulas, and with each question came a quick and effective response. One of the key indicators of the health of the system was that the IT team was not distracted into producing outputs from the system for the audit. This was all handled by the analysts and the business users, leaving the IT team free to focus on extending the platform and adding additional features. John and Harry were relieved to be in the job of building and leveraging technology again and not hand-holding broken processes.

A week after the submission, all checks and balances had been run, and the submission was approved. Everyone breathed a sigh of relief. The numbers had been cross-checked against other reports. Originally, this was a complex process, as the data had been transformed based on incompatible groupings and hierarchies. The new schema enabled them to validate the underlying granular numbers as well as to explain differences in the categorised reports. This gave them transparency and flexibility in what rules they used to build aggregations. Should there be investigations in the future, then the users would be able to provide valid reasons why the numbers were different. The schema would maintain its state at all points in time, making it easy to recreate and interrogate the reports from the past.

Jennifer was happy. The sheer lack of drama was something that she had wanted all along. No more late support nights for her, just ambitious and organised plans to deliver the IT systems that would empower and enable the business.

Her regular meeting with Mark was coming up. This would be the last of the sessions that they had put in place when the pressure had come on. They would return to a more normal meeting schedule going forwards. She took her usual seat in Mark's office at the designated time. Mark was not there; however, Tina had confirmed that he was on his way.

She opened her notebook and started writing down thoughts on the next few sprints as she waited. Five minutes later, Mark arrived with a big smile on his face. She was not sure what was on his mind.

"Hi, Jennifer, I hope all is well." He took a seat next to hers on the left-hand side. "What is on the agenda today?" he asked.

"Hi, Mark," she looked down at her notes. There was little to report other than business as usual.

"The team are focussed on extending the platform and bringing in more data from other sources. Harry is working on improving the self-service capabilities of the platform and creating the means to incorporate more flexibility in the configuration. We are reporting out lots of data-quality issues that Brian is now aware of. He is lobbying the data owners of the upstream systems, backed with evidence, to start improving their game. Other than that, it is business as usual. I have been monitoring the support calls in the system. There are now fewer severity 1 outages, and third-line support have not been called out for three weeks solid. The data-quality firewall and support procedures mean that the issues are being trapped early, fixed, and then rerun. The morale on the team is significantly higher than it has been in the past."

"The turnaround has been quicker than even I imagined," Mark said. "The work that you have done to change the direction and the trajectory of the team cannot be overestimated. I have just come from a meeting discussing the status of the regulatory submission, and there is genuine appreciation of what has been done. You deserve a lot of credit for this, Jennifer, along with the team. As a way of thanks, I have arranged for a night out for the whole team and all the stakeholders to celebrate the effort. The whole team will be invited, from both the business and IT. Brian has agreed to go joint on it."

Jennifer did not know what to think. She felt like they were only a short distance down the journey to what could be achieved by following the vision. She felt a little bit like it was too early to celebrate. They had got the submission out, but it would be a while before they were totally happy that it would be accepted by the regulator. On the other hand, the team had worked really hard, and for them to embrace something new and make a success of it so quickly was worth celebrating. The relationship with the business, and therefore the enthusiasm for the work, had improved significantly.

"Thank you, Mark, that is really kind of you. The team will really appreciate it. It was a lot of pressure, and they showed real belief to deliver on the solution," Jennifer responded.

"How about yourself?" Mark asked.

Jennifer thought for a moment. "I was just doing my job. I just followed patterns and processes that I have learnt over time to deliver the best results. We are not really anywhere near to the potential that I can see the team achieving," she replied honestly.

"That may be the case, Jennifer, but the difference that the processes and patterns that you have followed to what went before is night and day. Before this, we never seemed to be able to please the users. We spent the whole time working out how we could manage them and their expectations. When we delivered a solution, it did not meet their requirements, and they ended up doing the work themselves. You should not underestimate the difference that a few patterns and processes has had on the teams involved," Mark said.

"Thank you, Mark, I do not know what to say," Jennifer replied.

"You don't have to say anything, Jennifer. I have put you forward for a fast-track programme for the brightest and the most talented people in the organisation. The purpose of this is to make sure that you have the skills and experience necessary to climb the ladder and have a bigger impact on the organisation. The programme starts in a month's time and will contain the brightest and the best talent within the company."

"Thank you, Mark, that is amazing," Jennifer replied.

"It is deserved," Mark replied.

Jennifer was genuinely thrilled at the opportunity. She knew about the pro-gramme and the fact that senior management had many people who had been on the programme. It was seen across the industry as a fast track to the top.

The meeting naturally ended, and Jennifer returned to her desk.

Within a few minutes of her returning to her desk, the announcements started flowing over the email, first from the CEO on how the bank had pulled out all the stops and delivered on the promises to implement improvements in its regulatory submissions. It thanked all involved for their efforts to restore the reputation of the Saturn brand.

Following this was a message from the CRO, giving his thanks for the effort of the departments involved in preparing the submission and validating it to be correct. Then the email from Mark, which was the one that Jennifer was really looking for, acknowledging the team and Jennifer's recent appointment and how they had turned around a difficult position and come out on top. At the end of the message, there was a pointer towards leveraging the technologies that had been used on the Aspen project and implementing new ways of working across IT: "The success was due to the approach and the knowledge of the team and its leaders."

Jennifer felt a deep sense of pride in reading the email for the team and the journey they had been on and she would continue to push forward.

Within a minute, a second email sent from Mark came through to her inbox. This time it was a personal thanks to the team, containing the details of the night out. He had spared no expense—they were headed to Aqua Shard. They had booked out the restaurant and the bar at the top of the building for the teams that had delivered the project.

Jennifer immediately called together her teams through Justin, Dan, Ian, and Carl, asking them to meet inside the large conference room on the IT floor. She wanted to personally thank them all for showing such faith in the methods and the approach that she had pushed for.

She headed across to Justin's desk on the way to the meeting room. From here she could gather the leadership team together to head to the room. It took five minutes or so for all the teams to make it to the room. Jennifer, Justin, Carl, Ian, John, and Harry all gathered at the front of the room. There was not enough room for all the team to sit, so some stood around the edges behind the seats.

Jennifer started everything off. "Hi all, thanks for coming to this meeting at short notice. I will keep it brief. You will have seen from the emails being sent around today that our work over the last few months has made a big difference to Saturn. We had the lens on us, and we have delivered under high pressure and on time. The outcome is that the business has been able to make a confident submission to the regulator. It is early days to celebrate, but the confidence in the numbers and the platform are high. That is down to the hard work of everyone in this room and all the other people involved. We have changed the approach to data, and it is being recognised across the organisation. As way of thanks, Mark and Brian are hosting a big night out to celebrate the effort put in and the successful submission. We will all be going to the Aqua Shard for dinner and cocktails." She paused to allow the news to sink in.

"I would like to personally thank all of you for the support that you have given me since I took responsibility for this area. You have shown patience and faith in the DataOps approach, and I am pleased that we are all seeing the benefit of it now. There is a long way to go to fully implement the vision, but I could not be happier with the progress we have made to date." Jennifer looked around the room and saw a lot of smiling faces. "Justin, do you want to say a few words?"

Justin thought for a minute and then took a breath. "The challenge that we had at the beginning of this project seemed insurmountable. With our old ways of working, we were spending too long supporting processes and not enough time building an IT system. The approach that we are now following seems a million miles from where we were. I feel the morale in the room has lifted considerably, and the confidence to deliver has really shifted. I see people feeling more fulfilled from the direct team feedback that we are getting from the users. The momentum of the changes that we are delivering has reached levels we have never seen," he paused. "Reiterating what Jennifer said, this is down to the hard work of everyone here. We should really go out and enjoy ourselves and celebrate what we have achieved to date. Let us make this one night of many to come," Justin concluded.

Carl and Ian both took their turns to thank the teams and point them towards the future, and then the meeting disbanded. Jennifer headed back to her office with a warm glow of satisfaction.

• • •

On the night of the party, management had given the team the opportunity to leave early and prepare. Many of the team were dressing up in evening wear. This was going to be a big night. It was unusual for the bank to throw a big party—gone were the days of the huge expense budgets.

Jennifer managed to get home and change. She wanted to have a shower and switch from work mode into evening fun. She had the perfect dress for the party, which made her feel like a million dollars.

The journey back into central London on the tube was always a self-conscious affair. Most of the commuters were just wearing their work clothes and wanting to get home. Thankfully, the London Bridge tube station was on the line that she normally caught.

She walked around the back of the station, following the signs for the Shard. At the entrance, there was a VIP lane that was signed with the Saturn banking group, and there in the queue stood Brian in his black tie, looking very smart.

"Hi, Brian, you look great," Jennifer said with a big grin.

"Hi, Jennifer, you too," Brian said. "Are you looking forward to tonight?"

"Yes, we do not often get the opportunity to let our hair down and celebrate our successes," Jennifer replied.

"It's not that bad, is it?" Brian asked.

"No, but a lot of the team have historically put in heroic effort and largely for no real tangible success. The releases that they made were not used to their full potential, and the process of building solutions lost some of its soul," Jennifer replied.

"That can't be said for Aspen," Brian commented.

"No, through a combination of smart goals and targeted changes, I think the team are really starting to enjoy the job again. It is great to see them interacting with your team and solving problems together. It has given them a real lift and energy. It is much easier to manage them when they have enthusiasm every day for what they are doing," Jennifer said.

"I agree—the difference has been huge. If we had carried on how we were going, I would have had no faith in our ability to hit the deadline using the IT system. The project has really restored my faith in the whole process," Brian said.

They reached the front of the queue and entered security and on into the express lifts. Within two minutes they had reached the top of the building. The doors opened and Jennifer looked out and saw several of her team at the bar collecting drinks. She looked up and saw the view over the whole of the London skyline. It was going to be a great night!

Closing Questions

Realising DataOps is going to take some effort; the rewards outweigh that effort and, in my experience, will accumulate significantly. Here are some questions to think about:

- Are the teams around the data solutions collaborating effectively?
- Does each iteration take you closer to the destination?
- Are the users fans of the solution that you are producing?
- Is the data solution being built making a real impact on the business outcomes?
- Are the teams happy and engaged?

Part III

Appendix

Epilogue

JENNIFER IS waiting outside of the conference room on the business floor alongside Justin and Ian. It has been six months since the Aspen submission party. The steering committee is about to start for the Aspen project. Brian and the team are all gathered, along with Mark and Karen. The sessions have become a great meeting of minds. The business team, IT team, and CDO office are spending their time sharing their challenges and working through possible solutions. The flow of information and ideas is productive, as they navigate the shared demands for accurate and timely information.

Jennifer reflected on the progress since the first regulatory deadline. For six months, they had every possible enquiry and check and balance thrown at them. Internal audit, not wanting to be seen to have missed a reporting error, were the first to check the systems and procedures, followed by an external audit in which the company auditors were also not wanting to be embarrassed. Next came an extended visit by the regulator.

During this period, the team had kept the day to day running, supported the various audits, and moved the platform forwards considerably. They had split the pipeline up into manageable chunks, which had made it possible to reduce the size of the incremental releases. They had added automated tests and checks to increase the release cadence to new levels. The UI team led by Harry had made releases and changes regularly on a two-week cycle. Most of the releases were related to platform enhancements, as the users had the capability to build new analytics and reporting through the managed interface. The changes that they could make were completed with full traceability and lineage.

The advantages had accumulated and were huge in comparison to where they had come from. The audits that previously would have been a break in development and an archeology endeavor were mostly handled directly by Brian's business team. Firstly, this had put the problem in the hands of the business, who knew the data intimately and would give an accurate account of the results.

Secondly, the business was able to use the IT managed system to generate the results and not recall a spreadsheet from a shared drive. All of this meant they could confidently provide the auditors with validated results and reconciliations and demonstrate alignment between risk and P&L.

The development teams had been shielded from the process and had largely got on with improving the platform. Jennifer and Mark had been called upon to explain the level of controls they had in place, because the number of changes had increased. This was one of the downsides of the ability the team now had. The speed of release had increased dramatically, leading to the conclusion, by those who were not attached to the project, that it was due to instability. The reality was that the release processes and the new architecture, which had split up the monolith into discrete, manageable chunks, was the culprit, and the happy set of users the result.

To fend off attempts from certain parties in IT who wanted to undermine the success, Jennifer had produced outputs of all the automated tests and reconciliations that were run as part of the standard release cycle. It was almost impossible to find holes in what had been produced. Each change was accurately documented, and each variation in the numbers was investigated and explained. They had got the release process down to a fine art. By using automation, they could, if it were prudent, make a change, run a full regression test, and validate the results in a few hours to be available for the business to sign off on. Through clever data models, all the results for each run were kept in a form that could be analysed at any point in time. All attempts to sabotage the progress had been confidently rebuked, and the naysayers had finally started to lose their voices.

Mark's position as CIO had been confirmed by the board, who were hugely impressed with the turnaround. Chris Way's flame was dying, and he had been left to focus on the interest rates business without all the reporting and analytics. The organisation was finally starting to see through his desire for empire over delivery.

As they stood and waited, Jennifer caught Karen's eye outside the meeting. She was again comfortable in her role. By backing Jennifer's approach and providing resource to improve the situation, she had saved her position. After the submission, Jennifer and the team were able to focus on the requirements that the CDO office had for control. The automated data-quality reports were able to highlight all the issues with the upstream data. Most issues had workarounds built into the flow. The workarounds had been put together by data mappings that the users could configure with a workflow process. Although not ideal, it was a controlled solution that the auditors were pleased with; it had replaced the Excel® spreadsheets that had compensated before. The reports were providing all the information required in a form that could be quickly prioritised for the CDO, Brian, and Mark to address the data-quality issues. Rather than the regulatory reporting and information systems having to add layers and layers of workarounds, the attention had shifted upstream, and the systems feeding the reporting systems had a backlog of work that they had to fix.

Jennifer was due to give an update on the progress of the system at the steering committee. It was a great opportunity to describe how far they had come. With systems development, it was easy to get sucked into a cycle of feeling like you are never achieving. This was brought about by the constant demand for improvement. This was considerably enhanced when what you were doing was seen to be very successful. One of her favorite phrases was, "If you build it, they will come," paraphrased from the film "Field of Dreams," and was typical of all successful IT systems. As soon as it is built and in place, then the pressure would come on to do more and more. Her experience with data systems and analytics systems was that this happened more than with any other type of system. People's hunger for information only ever increases when they have access to it. The risk summary report of today quickly becomes the question of what-if scenarios tomorrow. Jennifer had learnt this lesson the hard way, and hence Aspen had fully implemented the extensibility that she had discussed together with Justin at the beginning of the project.

They had implemented the improvements to remove the technical debt in the project after the submission release. The technical iterations had enabled them to build extensibility in the system. The extensibility was built up of scalable, discrete components that could be reused and tested independently. Having a micro services architecture enabled the team to update components and change their purpose independently of other processes if they left the defined interface that other services relied on in place. The data models that Dan and Carl had provided the tech team were enabling them to slot new requirements in with consistent datasets and reuse data from previous iterations.

All of this was supported by the metadata that they had now collected and arranged from the existing data processes and the analysis phases of projects. The metadata hub had a collation of lots of provenance and lineage, as well as a clear set of terms that mapped onto physical tables and fields. They had built up a large collection of instrumentation that provided them with sizes, numbers of rows, and other profiling data. It was enabling them to more accurately architect, size, and configure the system and the underlying infrastructure. This enabled them to provide more accurate costing information back to the steering group, who would decide on the merits of the requirements that they were asking for.

On the agenda for today's steering meeting was the expansion of the team. The success of Aspen meant that more responsibility was being pushed towards the business team and Jennifer and the IT team. The bank was wanting to use the platform for its finance reporting and treasury reporting. Jennifer thought to herself that it would be possible, but some thought needed to go into making sure that the system would not get snarled up in cross-dependencies and require-ments bottlenecks.

Jennifer was finally starting to feel proud of her achievements. She had felt a bit of a fraud after the submission, as a very small amount of work had been done compared to what she knew was possible. Now it was six months later, and most of the patterns and processes had been implemented across the team. They were in a rhythm of doing the right things, and they now had the experience to keep it going forwards, with her only making small touches on the rudder.

She had joined the fast track for the best talent in the bank. She had attended lots of one-day events, as well as a week-long offsite. The offsite had been with a theme on leading teams. It had lots of activities to reinforce and extend her knowledge and experience. In every session and event, she had made new friends, and she was learning more and more.

Mark had created a specific role for her in the organisation that granted her the authority and the influence to start changing how the organisation was approaching data. She was focused from the IT side, and Karen, the CDO, was the lead from the business side. They were in charge of updating the standard methodology into Six Pillar (see Figure A.1 on following page). The pillars were described as the IMPACT pillars due to the impact the changes were having on the organisation.

I. **I** was for Instrumentation brought about through the lean methodology of continuous improvement. By monitoring every step in the manufactur-ing process and using this to drive quality and improvement, the resulting product at the end of the production line would be high quality. In the case of Aspen, this was the work that Carl Hinkley and Dan Churchill had driven. By profiling and instrumenting data, they could make sure that the solution would fit what they needed.

II. **M** was for Metadata—the data that they captured in Aspen through the Instrumentation organised into a metadata hub. By focusing on this and making sure the metadata captured sizes and flow information as well as data-quality outputs, the team would be able to see the flow from the 1,000-foot viewpoint. The information was being used to improve the existing process and to influence future projects.

III. **P** was for Platforms. The key to the Aspen platform was architecting it dynamically and making it extensible. By Jennifer's working with Justin, Dan, Harry, and John to reorganise the layout of the data and the archi-tecture, they had built a system that could scale and iterate to the Target incrementally. If they had kept the monolith, then those iterations would not have met the needs of the users or the cycles that information systems typically go through.

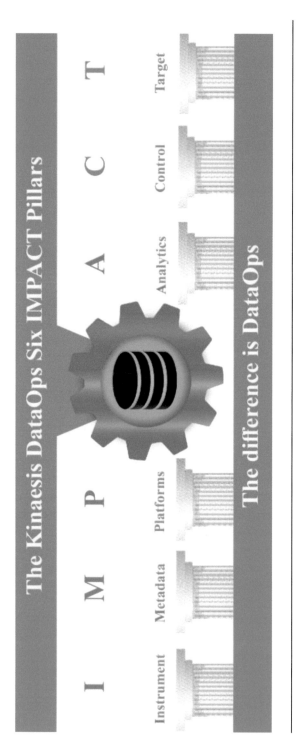

Figure A.1   The Six IMPACT Pillars of DataOps.

IV. **A** was for Analytics, but in DataOps it is for collaborative analytics. Designing a system for the users was key to their wanting to use it, which would focus their energy on the quality and functionality of the system. In the monolith, the users only wanted to extract the data from the system to get what they needed. All the energy was then spent on the extracted data and not the system. This was the way that Jennifer had seen many data systems die. By letting go and meeting the users' needs, Aspen kept the energy and the input focused on improvements to the solution.

V. **C** would stand for Control. With Aspen, the key to controlling what people did was to make sure that they were empowered within a framework. The democratisation of the Aspen system came by the facilitation of information that described the quality of the data and by aligning the maintenance of the metadata to the outcomes that added value to the supply chain. By linking the glossaries and dictionaries through to the reporting and connecting them to the requirements process, then they would be lovingly maintained by those who then see the output every day. The side effect of this is a well-described and maintained set of information that can be bundled and leveraged for control and for answering the regulatory questions.

VI. **T** was for Target. It comes at the end of the IMPACT pillars, as it describes the destination for the DataOps journey. However, its roots are put down at the beginning. By describing the correct destination at the start of the journey, then the outcome is achievable. By ignoring what the users really need and focusing on columns in reports only, the soul of the data system is ignored, and therefore the quality of the effort being put into the specification is low. Errors introduced at the start are amplified significantly when the journey reaches its end. Jennifer had started here along with Ian.

Karen and Jennifer set out the Six IMPACT Pillars on a roadmap for future success at Saturn. They worked them into the existing IT development methodology, where they made sense by introducing the missing elements. They thought that this would be the best method for them to evolve the culture of development rather than to revolutionise it. Over time, the improvement in data practices would enable Saturn to make informed decisions and help its customers with more targeted and personal services.

All revolutions are an accumulation of small steps in the right direction.